Our Way 3

PREMIUM EDITION

AMOS
PRESCHER
PASQUALIN

Richmond

Richmond

Diretoria: *Paul Berry*
Gerência editorial: *Sandra Possas*
Coordenação de arte: *Christiane Borin*
Coordenação de *bureau*: *Américo Jesus*
Coordenação de revisão: *Katia Gouveia Vitale*
Gerência de produção gráfica: *André Monteiro*
Coordenação de produção gráfica: *Maria de Lourdes Rodrigues*
Gerência de produção industrial: *Wilson Aparecido Troque*

Coordenação do projeto: *Adriana Beatriz Saporito, Ana Lucia Militello, Henrique Zanardi*

Edição de texto: *Adriana Beatriz Saporito, Henrique Zanardi*
Assistência editorial: *Bruna Marini, Camila Carmo da Silva, Kelly Taniguchi, Mariana Zanini, Nathália Horvath*
Preparação de texto: *Maria Estela de Alcântara, Thelma Guimarães*
Revisão linguística: *Raymond Shoulder*
Revisão: *Alexandre Gomes Camarú, Juliana Sant'Ana Cavalcanti de Queiroz, Mariana Mininel de Almeida, Rafael Gustavo Spigel, Vivian Marques Viccino, Viviane Mendes*
Projeto gráfico e edição de arte: *David Urbinatti Netto*
Ilustrações: *Airon Barreto, Eduardo Medeiros*
Criações: *Amanda Savoini, Gisele A. Rocha, Hulda Melo, Talita Guedes, Tangente Design*
Capa: *Amanda Savoini*
Pesquisa iconográfica: *Carol Böck, Marcia Sato, Mariana Veloso Lima*
Tratamento de imagens: *Arleth Rodrigues, Fabio N. Precendo, Pix Art, Wagner Lima*
Diagramação: *Tangente Design*
Pré-impressão: *Alexandre Petreca, Everton L. de Oliveira Silva, Hélio P. de Souza Filho, Marcio H. Kamoto*
Impressão e acabamento: TypeBrasil

Welcome Unit: *Luciana Pimentel*
Extra Reading: *Luciana Silva*
Grammar Reference: *Carla Maurício Coelho da Silva Vianna*
Manual do professor: *Luciana Silva, Nelson Mitrano Neto*

Dados Internacionais de Catalogação na Publicação (CIP)
(Câmara Brasileira do Livro, SP, Brasil)

Amos, Eduardo
Our way / Eduardo Amos, Elisabeth Prescher, Ernesto Pasqualin. – 7. ed. – São Paulo : Moderna, 2012.

Obra em 4 v. para alunos do 6º ao 9º ano do ensino fundamental.

1. Inglês (Ensino fundamental) 2. Inglês (Ensino fundamental) – Atividades, exercícios etc. I. Prescher, Elisabeth. II. Pasqualin, Ernesto. III. Título.

12-05155 CDD-372.652

Índices para catálogo sistemático:
1. Inglês : Ensino fundamental 372.652

ISBN 978-85-16-07942-0 (LA)
ISBN 978-85-16-07943-7 (LP)

RICHMOND
EDITORA MODERNA LTDA.
Rua Padre Adelino, 758 - Belenzinho
São Paulo - SP - Brasil - CEP 03303-904
Central de atendimento ao usuário: 0800 771 8181
www.richmond.com.br
2015

Impresso no Brasil

Créditos das fotos:
Capa: © Idea for life/Shutterstock
P. 7: © KC Hunter/Alamy/Other Images; © Supri Suharjoto/Shutterstock; © Michael Hitoshi/Getty Images; © Thinkstock/Getty Images; © Thinkstock/Getty Images; P. 8: © Marcel Antonisse/AFP Photo/Getty Images; P. 11: © Helga Esteb/Shutterstock; © Jean-Marc Loubat/Gamma-Rapho/Getty Images; © Kevin Mazur/WireImage/Getty Images; © Sean Gallup/Getty Images; © NBC/Everett Collection/Grupo Keystone; © Thinkstock/Getty Images; © Thinkstock/Getty Images; © Zumapress/Diomedia; © Bettmann/Corbis/Latinstock; P. 16: © Thinkstock/Getty Images; P. 17: © Bettmann/Corbis/Latinstock; © Album/Latinstock; © Interfoto/Latinstock P. 24: © Andresr/Shutterstock; © Robynrg/Shutterstock; © Charles Taylor/Shutterstock; © Lane V. Erickson/Shutterstock; © Thinkstock/Getty Images; © Ghenadie/Shutterstock; © Robynrg/Shutterstock; © Marcus Miranda/Shutterstock; © Defpicture/Shutterstock; P. 26: © Tarsila do Amaral Empreendimentos – Museu de Arte Contemporânea da Universidade de São Paulo, São Paulo, SP; © Tarsila do Amaral Empreendimentos – Fundação José e Paulina Nemirowsky, São Paulo, SP; © Tarsila do Amaral Empreendimentos – Museu Hermitage, São Petersburgo, Rússia; P. 28: © Michael Steele/Getty Images; P. 31: © Valeriy Velikov/Shutterstock; © StockLite/Shutterstock; © Yellowj/Shutterstock; © Zurijeta/Shutterstock; © Losevsky Photo and Video/Shutterstock; © The Image Bank/Getty Images; P. 37: © Bettmann/Corbis/Latinstock; © Bettmann/Corbis/Latinstock; © SuperStock/Getty Images; P. 41: © Universal Images Group/DeAgostini/Alamy/Other Images; © Gary Yim/Shutterstock; © FPG/Archive Photos/Getty Images; P. 42: © Ildi Papp/Shutterstock; © Zirconicusso/Shutterstock; © Oleksiy Mark/Shutterstock; © Vibrant Image Studio/Shutterstock; © Ljupco Smokovski/Shutterstock; © Ljupco Smokovski/Shutterstock; © Dasha Petrenko/Shutterstock; © Nayashkova Olga/Shutterstock; © Taina Sohlman/Shutterstock; © Mats Bergström/Shutterstock; P. 44: © Mark Van Overmeire/Shutterstock; © Departamento de Filatelia e Produtos/ECT; P. 47: © Time & Life Pictures/Getty Images; P. 56: © Graça Victoria/Shutterstock; © Nuzsy/Shutterstock; © Thinkstock/Getty Images; © Monkey Business Images/Shutterstock; P. 58: Wollertz/Shutterstock; P. 60: © S Bukley/Shutterstock; © Helga Esteb/Shutterstock; © Paulo Resende/Shutterstock; © Globetrotter J/Shutterstock; © S Bukley/Shutterstock; © S Bukley/Shutterstock; P. 63: © Thinkstock/Getty Images; © Mooboyba/Shutterstock; © Thinkstock/Getty Images; © Ron Hilton/Shutterstock; © Thinkstock/Getty Images; © Thinkstock/Getty Images; P. 66: Olga Bogatyrenko/Shutterstock; © Forestpath/Shutterstock; P. 68: © Christopher Ray Robertson/Shutterstock; P. 71: © Cartoonstock; P. 72: © Gorilla/Shutterstock; © Andresr/Shutterstock; © Auremar/Shutterstock; © PT Images/Shutterstock; © Nailia Schwarz/Shutterstock; © Thinkstock/Getty Images; P. 73: © Thinkstock/Getty Images; © Thinkstock/Getty Images; © Thinkstock/Getty Images; © Thinkstock/Getty Images; © Thinkstock/Getty Images; © Mike Tan C T/Shutterstock; © LeonP/Shutterstock; © Matt Jeppson/Shutterstock; © Thinkstock/Getty Images; P. 74: © Monika Wisniewska/Shutterstock; © Eric Isselée/Shutterstock; © NinaMalyna/Shutterstock; P. 77: © Duncan Selby/Alamy/Other Images; © PA Wire/Press Association Images/Other Images; © The Bridgeman Art Library/Grupo Keystone/The Munch-Museum The Munch-Ellingsen Group/Licenciado por AUTVIS, Brasil, 2012; © AFP Photo/Getty Images; P. 78: © Thinkstock/Getty Images; © Buzz Pictures/Alamy/Other Images; © Thinkstock/Getty Images; P. 79: © Thinkstock/Getty Images; © Kilerus/Shutterstock; © Wdeon/Shutterstock; P. 80: Alexandre Chacon; P. 82: © Catherinka/Shutterstock; © CGissemann/Shutterstock; © Thinkstock/Getty Images; © Bouzou/Shutterstock; © Donatas1205/Shutterstock; © Thinkstock/Getty Images; © Thinkstock/Getty Images; © Photographer's Choice/Getty Images; P. 87: © Reprodução; P. 88: YanLev/Shutterstock; © Thinkstock/Getty Images; © Andresr/Shutterstock; P. 89: © Hippo/Shutterstock; © Bojanovic/Shutterstock; © Oviii/Shutterstock; © Tristan Tan/Shutterstock; © Bojanovic/Shutterstock; © Charobnica/Shutterstock; © Gabrielle Ewart/Shutterstock; © Nicholas Piccillo/Shutterstock; © ChromaCo/Shutterstock; P. 90: © Silva Junior/Folha Imagem; © Roberto Vazquez/Futura Press; P. 92: Renato Soares/Pulsar Imagens; © Marcelo Spatafora/Pulsar Imagens; © Paulo Fridman/Pulsar Imagens; P. 94: © Éric Isselée/Shutterstock; P. 95: © Thinkstock/Getty Images; © Thinkstock/Getty Images; © João Prudente/Pulsar Imagens; P. 106: © Cinemafestival/Shutterstock; P. 118: © Thinkstock/Getty Images; © Topseller/Shutterstock; P. 119: Goodluz/Shutterstock.

Contents

Welcome Unit	4
1 I Was Surprised	8
2 There Was a Town Here	18
3 Running in the Dark	28
4 We Went to Brasília	38
5 In the Media	48
6 Healthy Salad	58
7 Man's Best Friend	68
8 Skydiving	78
Extra Readings	88
Grammar Reference	96
Workbook	105
Glossary	121
Irregular Verbs	134
Track List	136

Welcome Unit

Friends around the World

At the mall...
What do you usually do on the weekends in Spain, Juan?
Well, Koji, I hang out with my friends, go to the movies and play video games.
What time do you go to school in Spain?
School starts at 8 a.m. and ends at 3 p.m.
What do you do after school in Spain, Juan?
On Mondays and Wednesdays I play soccer and on Tuesdays and Thursdays I have English classes.
Do you want to watch this movie, Juan?
Sure, Koji! This is a horror movie and the leading actor is my favorite!
The Haunted Mountain
TICKETS
So, let's go to the movies!
Cool! Let's go!

1 Check Yes or No.

	Yes	No
1 Koji is Spanish.	☐	☐
2 Agostina isn't Japanese.	☐	☐
3 Agostina is Koji's sister.	☐	☐
4 Koji is on an exchange program in Spain.	☐	☐
5 Juan is in Australia right now.	☐	☐
6 Juan and Koji are classmates.	☐	☐
7 Koji and Juan are going to school.	☐	☐

2 Correct the wrong sentences in exercise 1.

____

____

____

____

3 Match the columns.

1 In Spain, Juan plays	a ☐	at the mall.
2 In Spain, Juan has English classes	b ☐	horror movies.
3 Juan likes	c ☐	soccer after school.
4 Juan and Koji are	d ☐	on Tuesdays and Thursdays.

4 Answer the questions.

1 Who is Koji talking to on the computer?

____

2 Why doesn't Agostina have classes today?

____

3 What are Juan's parents doing?

____

4 What does Juan do on the weekends in Spain?

____

5 How long does Juan spend at school every day in Spain?

____

5 Listen to the dialogues. Number the pictures according to what you hear.

a

b

c

d

e

6 Find 5 verbs in the wordsearch.

Y	R	Y	Q	K	L	W	V	X	Y	M	W	P	W	D
Q	E	Q	M	W	I	U	Z	C	L	G	N	U	L	K
U	B	U	X	Y	K	B	W	Y	K	H	K	M	I	F
C	W	Q	K	N	E	S	I	Z	Y	D	E	J	J	E
M	O	Y	O	B	M	A	R	Y	N	Z	X	Z	D	Z
I	V	M	X	K	H	M	P	O	L	I	F	E	D	R
D	F	E	E	M	D	U	P	V	J	O	D	A	W	E
E	J	J	T	Z	T	A	P	E	H	F	X	Z	V	Y
M	A	E	W	K	F	W	J	O	Y	L	S	A	O	K
A	G	K	O	S	B	U	Y	Q	O	K	H	D	S	K
Z	L	B	T	U	M	N	T	W	L	J	D	E	K	I
H	X	S	V	K	W	E	Q	X	C	T	L	D	R	E
Z	M	E	A	I	H	J	D	F	H	T	H	Y	I	X
B	E	M	E	J	F	M	P	A	G	K	Y	T	A	L
X	Y	R	J	S	A	M	Q	S	F	C	F	W	L	S

1 I Was Surprised

1 Look at the text and answer.

1 What kind of text is this?

2 Who is the text about?

3 **2** Read the text about a girl named Thandiwe Chama.

Address: http://listverse.com

Search

Wed
July 16, 2008

7 Children Who Changed the World

192 comments

Thandiwe Chama

Thandiwe Chama was born on February 15, 1991 in Lusaka, Zambia. When she was eight years old, her school was closed because there were no teachers. She was very angry and protested. Thandiwe and sixty other children walked a long way to find another school. She was their leader. A few weeks later, another school accepted the children.

In 2007, the International Children's Peace Prize was presented to Thandiwe in the city The Hague. The prize consists of a statuette – The Nkosi – and 100,000 euros to be used in an aid project in her community. That was an important day in her life and her speech was really impressive.

In her blog, Thandiwe writes about that day: "I was surprised that I was crying. I was nervous but they were also tears of joy. Here in Zambia it is difficult, especially for a girl, to stand up and say something. I was pleased that the people were impressed with my story and they even asked a lot of questions."

Today, Thandiwe fights for children's rights to education. She also speaks about Aids in churches and other public places.

Learn more about Thandiwe Chama in her blog at <http://thandiwechama.blogspot.com>.

Based on: <http://listverse.com>. Accessed on: April 30, 2012.

3 Match the columns according to the text.

1 1991 — a ( ) Year of publication of the article.
2 1999 — b ( ) Thandiwe received the International Children's Peace Prize.
3 2007 — c ( ) Thandiwe's school was closed.
4 2008 — d ( ) Thandiwe was born.

4 Answer the questions about the text on page 8.

1 When was the article published?

___

2 What does the number 192 mean?

___

3 What is the title of the article?

___

4 In what year was Thandiwe's school closed?

___

5 Thandiwe received the International Children's Peace Prize. Why? (Answer in Portuguese.)

___

___

5 Find in the text four words that express Thandiwe's feelings at the ceremony in The Hague. Complete the sentence below.

She was ___, ___, ___ and ___.

6 Challenge.

1 The title of the text is "7 Children Who Changed the World". Thandiwe Chama is one of them. Find the names of the other six on the internet.

2 The approximate population in Zambia.

3 The languages people speak in Zambia.

Let's Talk about It

A escola de Thandiwe foi fechada por falta de professores. Thandiwe, então, decidiu lutar por seus direitos e protestou firmemente. Qual é a sua opinião a respeito da atitude dela? No nosso dia a dia, quais atitudes podemos tomar para construir um mundo mais igualitário?

7 Look at the pictures. Practice the conversations.

1

at home / two hours ago

A: *Was he at home two hours ago?*

B: *Yes, he was.*

A: *Were they at work last night?*

B: *No, they weren't.*

2

at work / last night

3

at the restaurant / yesterday

4

in the park / last Monday

5

at school / on Friday

6

in the yard / in the afternoon

7

in the office / this morning

8

at the store / three hours ago

8 Talk to a classmate about the famous people below.

1

Elizabeth Taylor – actress
February 27, 1932
London, England

A: *When was Elizabeth Taylor born?*
B: *She was born on February 27, 1932.*
A: *Where was she born?*
B: *She was born in London, England.*
A: *What was her occupation?*
B: *She was an actress.*

2

Ayrton Senna – racing car driver
March 21, 1960
São Paulo, Brazil

3

Michael Jackson – pop singer
August 29, 1958
Gary, Indiana, U.S.

4

Steve Jobs – inventor
February 24, 1955
San Francisco, California, U.S.

5

Amy Winehouse – singer
September 14, 1983
London, England

6

Cleopatra – Egyptian Queen
The year 69 B.C.
Alexandria, Egypt

7

Leonardo da Vinci – painter
April 15, 1452
Vinci, Italy

8

Albert Einstein – physicist
March 14, 1879
Ulm, Germany

9

Agatha Christie – writer
September 15, 1890
Torquay, England

GRAMMAR

To be – Simple Past

I **was**	**Affirmative:**	The teacher **was** in the classroom five minutes ago.
You **were**	**Negative:**	Amelia **was not** at the shopping mall yesterday afternoon.
He **was**		
She **was**	**Interrogative:**	**Were** the engineers at the company last Saturday?
It **was**	**Short answers:**	Yes, they **were**. / No, they **weren't**.
We **were**	**Contracted form:**	was not = **wasn't** / were not = **weren't**
You **were**		
They **were**		

Expressões geralmente usadas com o *Simple Past*: *yesterday*, *last*, *ago*.

9 Unscramble the words to form sentences.

1 in / were / They / last / town / week / .

____

2 yesterday / he / tired / Was / ?

____

3 Monday / weren't / last / busy / We / .

____

10 Rewrite the sentences below. Use the Simple Past and the adverbs given.

1 I am very nervous today. (yesterday)

I was very nervous yesterday.

2 Doris is busy now. (two hours ago)

____

3 They aren't at work right now. (last Monday)

____

4 Larry isn't at school today. (last week)

____

11 Ask questions for the answers below.

1 Where ______________________________?

The cat was on the roof.

2 When ______________________________?

Mr. and Mrs. Geller were in Spain last week.

3 Who ______________________________?

Dan was Kelly's boyfriend.

12 Read the text below. Use the Simple Past of the verb *to be* to complete it.

Yesterday it ______________ very hot. The Smiths ______________ on their farm. Ronald ______________ in the lake with his sister and his mom ______________ in the pool. His father ______________ in the barn. Their dog ______________ near the lake. They ______________ very happy there.

4 **13** Listen to a dialogue. Check the correct answers.

1 How many people are involved in this conversation?

ⓐ ☐ Two.
ⓑ ☐ Three.
ⓒ ☐ Four.

2 Where are they now?

ⓐ ☐ At a party.
ⓑ ☐ At the beach.
ⓒ ☐ At home.

3 Where were they last night?

ⓐ ☐ At a party.
ⓑ ☐ At the beach.
ⓒ ☐ At home.

4 Linda, Jack, Bob and their friends were at a party last night. Bob was

ⓐ ☐ near the garden.
ⓑ ☐ close to the living room.
ⓒ ☐ near the pool.

5 **14** Listen to the sentences. Check where the people below were.

	LIVING ROOM	POOL	BEDROOM	GARDEN
Jack				
Linda				
Anna				
Anna's mother				

15 Write two sentences about each of the famous people on page 11.

1 ____________________

2 ____________________

3 ____________________

4 ____________________

5 ____________________

6 ____________________

7 ____________________

8 ____________________

9 ____________________

16 There is a prize in your community: "Kids for a Better World". Write a letter to the Prize Committee and nominate a kid you know. Write his / her name and the reasons why he / she deserves to win the prize.

____________________ (date)

To: Prize Nomination Committee

From: ____________________ (your full name)

I wish to nominate (name of nominee) ____________________ for the prize Kids for a Better World because...

____________________ (signature)

FUN

17 Write in the crossword the places where David was last week. Then talk to a classmate.

A: *Where was David on Sunday?*

B: *He was at the restaurant.*

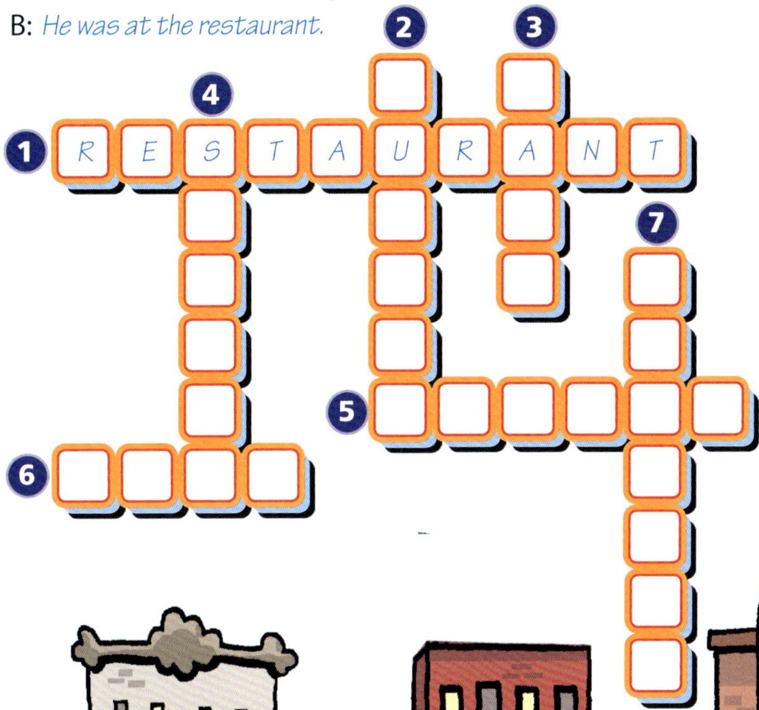

1 on Sunday
2 last Monday
3 on Tuesday
4 on Saturday
5 on Friday night
6 on Sunday night
7 on Thursday

Key Language

angry	long way	presented	publish
another	nomination	prize	speech
impressive	peace	protest	

Way to Go

1 Underline the correct alternatives.

1 My boss and I **were** / **was** at the new office yesterday. It's amazing!

2 Their Geography books **was** / **were** here a minute ago. They aren't anymore.

3 Dan **was** / **were** in the kitchen, but he **wasn't** / **weren't** cooking.

4 Sue and Pam **are** / **were** sleeping at the moment. They **are** / **were** very tired after the party yesterday.

5 Samantha **is** / **was** in Argentina now. Last month she and her family **are** / **were** in Peru.

2 Read the sentences below. Write T (true) or F (false). Correct the false ones.

1 ☐ Thomas Edison was a famous singer in the 19th century.

____

2 ☐ In 2002, the Brazil soccer team was world champion for the fifth time.

____

3 ☐ Rio de Janeiro was the capital of Brazil in the past.

____

4 ☐ Lula was elected Governor of São Paulo in 2002.

____

5 ☐ Barack Obama wasn't the winner of The Nobel Peace Prize in 2009.

____

3 Write questions for the underlined parts.

Mom was **(1)** <u>at the mall</u> with **(2)** <u>Aunt Clara</u> yesterday night. She was looking for **(3)** <u>a special gift for Dad</u>. But **(4)** <u>it wasn't her lucky day</u>, she found nothing. She and Aunt Clara were still **(5)** <u>frustrated</u> this morning!

1 ______________________________

2 ______________________________

3 ______________________________

4 ______________________________

5 ______________________________

4 Complete the dialogues with *was*, *wasn't*, *were* or *weren't*.

Jane: Where ____________ Picasso from?
Taylor: He ____________ from Spain. His first name was Pablo.
Jane: ____________ he an actor?
Taylor: No, he ____________. Please, Jane! He ____________ a painter.

Paul: John Lennon and Elvis Presley. I know these names. ____________ they actors?
Carol: No, they ____________. They were singers, Paul.
Paul: Oh, that's true! Where ____________ they from?
Carol: John Lennon ____________ from England and Elvis Presley ____________ from the United States.
Paul: I bet you are a music fan, Carol.

5 This is a form for a school project about students' childhood. Complete the questions using *was* or *were* and answer them.

1 What ____________ your first words?

____

2 What ____________ your favorite toy?

____

3 Who ____________ your first friend?

____

4 What ____________ your favorite food?

____

5 ____________ you a happy child?

____

2 There Was a Town Here

1 Look at the text and pictures and answer.

1 What kind of text is it?

2 What is the text about?

7 **2** Read about Luca and his grandfather.

3 Underline the correct answers. Explain your choice in Portuguese.

1	Luca was born in that region.	Yes.	No.	Probably not.
	Explain why: ______			
2	Luca and his grandfather are good friends.	Yes.	No.	Surely not.
	Explain why: ______			
3	The old man was born in that area.	Yes, certainly.	No.	Possibly.
	Explain why: ______			
4	It rains a lot in that area during summer.	Yes.	No.	Certainly.
	Explain why: ______			
5	The construction of the dam was a good thing.	Yes.	No.	I don't know.
	Explain why: ______			

Let's Talk about It

As pessoas se sentem entristecidas quando veem lugares importantes de suas vidas serem destruídos. Como você se sentiria nesse caso? Por quê? Quais são as consequências para a natureza quando uma represa é construída?

4 Look at the pictures and talk about the differences with a classmate. Use the words in the box.

bandstand buildings cars church houses parking lot theater

TODAY

SIXTY YEARS AGO

5 Write sentences about the pictures in exercise 4.

1 a theater *There wasn't a theater* sixty years ago. *There is a theater today.*

2 houses ______ sixty years ago. ______

3 a bandstand ______ sixty years ago. ______

4 cars ______ sixty years ago. ______

GRAMMAR

There to Be – Present and Past

Singular		Plural	
Present		**Present**	
There is: Há, existe		**There are:** Há, existem	
Affirmative:	**There is** a parking lot here.	**Affirmative:**	**There are** cars in the parking lot.
Interrogative:	**Is there** a church here?	**Interrogative:**	**Are there** cars in the parking lot?
Negative:	**There isn't** a theater here.	**Negative:**	**There aren't** cars in the parking lot.
Past		**Past**	
There was: Havia, existia		**There were:** Havia, existiam	
Affirmative:	**There was** a parking lot here.	**Affirmative:**	**There were** cars in the parking lot.
Interrogative:	**Was there** a church here?	**Interrogative:**	**Were there** cars in the parking lot?
Negative:	**There wasn't** a theater here.	**Negative:**	**There weren't** cars in the parking lot.

6 Read the chart. Then write T (true) or F (false).

YEAR	INVENTION/FACT	YEAR	INVENTION/FACT
1284	eyeglasses	1950	credit card
1858	washing machine	1953	color TV
1875	telephone	1969	bar-code scanner
1880	toilet paper	1974	home computer
1886	Coca-Cola	1988	digital cellular phone
1889	Eiffel Tower, Paris	2007	iPhone
1898	roller coaster	2010	Etna eruption, Italy
1920	Band-Aid	2011	Parapan American Games in Guadalajara, Mexico
1928	penicillin		

1 [ ] There was Coca-Cola in 1886.

2 [ ] There were eyeglasses in 1250.

3 [ ] There is penicillin nowadays.

4 [ ] There was a volcanic eruption in Italy in 2009.

5 [ ] There were home computers in 1970.

6 [ ] There were Parapan Games in Mexico in 2010.

7 [ ] After 1988 there was digital cell phone.

8 [ ] After 1953 there was color TV.

GRAMMAR

Personal Pronouns (review)

Subject Pronouns (usados como sujeito)	Object Pronouns (usados como objeto)
I	me
you	you
he	him
she	her
it	it
we	us
you	you
they	them

Sandy likes this dress.
She → it

Brad likes these CDs.
He → them

7 Check the appropriate alternative. Then, complete the dialogues.

1 **A:** Are Paul and Kelly coming to class now?

B: Yes, __________ are.

☐ them ☐ they

2 **A:** Does Ann talk to your brother every week?

B: No, __________ talks to __________ every day.

☐ she – them ☐ she – him

3 **A:** When do you meet your girlfriend?

B: __________ meet __________ on Saturdays.

☐ I – her ☐ Me – her

4 **A:** What is Charles going to give Darlene?

B: __________ is going to give __________ a bracelet.

☐ He – she ☐ He – her

8 There are mistakes in the sentences below. Rewrite and correct them.

1 There was many banks on this street.

There were many banks on this street. / There was a bank on this street.

2 Were there a mall near the square?

____

3 There weren't a girl behind me.

____

4 Was there children at the playground?

____

5 There wasn't students in the classroom.

____

8 9 Look, listen and circle the correct alternative.

1	number of ducks	Yes	No	6	number of boys	Yes	No
2	the woman	Yes	No	7	the boys	Yes	No
3	the man	Yes	No	8	the dog	Yes	No
4	the girls	Yes	No	9	the cats	Yes	No
5	the dark-haired girl	Yes	No	10	the birds	Yes	No

10 Read a note on the Lost and Found board at a school. Check the pictures.

I lost my schoolbag this morning.
Inside it there was a Math book, notebooks, a blue pen and a pink sharpener. There were also dollar bills ($5 and $20) and a pencil case.
If someone finds it, please keep it for me.

Joanne Keppler
8th grade

11 You have lost your schoolbag at school. Post a message on the school board.

FUN

12 Do the crossword.

1	It is popular in amusement parks.	7	You use it when you cut yourself.
2	It went home in 1974.	8	They took place in Guadalajara.
3	A volcano does it.	9	It washes clothes.
4	You use it to talk to people.	10	There is one in Paris.
5	Alex Flemming discovered it.	11	It is plastic money.
6	Life is difficult without it.	12	You wear them to see well.

9 Key Language

bandstand	building	dam	go down	over	scary	today
be afraid	certainly	dangerous	lake	possibly	school	tower
be born	church	exactly	main street	rain	square	town
branch	City Hall	fish	nowadays	reappear	theater	under

Way to Go

1 Read the dialogue below. Complete it with *there to be* in the appropriate verb tense.

Cynthia: Hi, Sophie! How was the visit to the museum yesterday afternoon?

Sophie: Hey, Cynthia. It was amazing! The museum has changed a lot. Some months ago ______________________ two rooms for Latin American artists' works of art. Now, ______________________ just one room for an exhibition of Tarsila do Amaral's paintings, my favorite Brazilian painter.

Cynthia: Really? ______________________ any other Brazilian paintings in this exhibition?

Sophie: No, ______________________ only Tarsila do Amaral's paintings.

Cynthia: In your opinion, what is her best painting?

Sophie: Well, I prefer "Carnaval em Madureira". Have you seen it?

Cynthia: I'm afraid not. Describe it to me.

Sophie: Well, ______________________ houses in it and some children and women, too. Oh, I almost forgot! ______________________ a huge tower in the middle of the painting, the Eiffel Tower!

Cynthia: Nice. ______________________ students from other schools visiting the museum yesterday?

Sophie: No, ______________________.

Cynthia: What about the teachers?

Sophie: ______________________ just one with us, Mrs. Spencer. She is a great Art teacher, you know.

Cynthia: Sure. I wish I had been there...

2 Read the dialogue in exercise 1 again. Check the painting *Carnaval em Madureira*.

☐

☐

☐

3 Substitute the underlined parts in the sentences below. Use Object Pronouns.

1 Can you help Janet and her kids?

____

2 Mandy doesn't meet Joseph and Joseph doesn't meet Mandy when they are too busy.

____

3 Here are the sandwiches and the juice. Eat the sandwiches and drink the juice.

____

4 Daniel and I are going to the movies. Do you want to go with me and Daniel?

____

10 **4** Read the text below. Fill in the blanks with words from the box. Then, listen and check your answers.

hormonal	oil free	puberty	remove	skin	washing

Address: http://kidshealth.org

Search

What Is Acne and What Causes It?

Acne is a condition of the ________ that teenagers have because of ________ changes that come with ________. If your parents had acne when they were teens, you'll probably have it too.

What Can I Do About Acne?

Oily skin can contribute to acne so wash your face once or twice a day. Don't scrub your face. It may irritate the skin and pores.

If you wear make-up or sunscreen, make sure it's ________. This means it won't clog your pores which contributes to acne. When you are ________ your face, be sure to ________ all of your make-up.

Based on: <http://kidshealth.org>. Accessed on: April 30, 2012.

5 Read the text from exercise 4 again. Then, answer the questions.

1 Teens have acne because of hormonal changes. What is the other reason besides that?

____

2 How often do you have to wash your face in order to prevent acne?

____

3 What is the consequence of scrubbing your face?

____

4 Why are oil free products better for the skin?

____

3 Running in the Dark

1 Look at the text. Discuss the questions below with your classmates.

1 What do you know about the Paralympic Games?

2 Do you know anyone with special needs?

11 **2** Read about a very special Brazilian athlete.

Sports Illustrated

Ádria Rocha dos Santos

Picture yourself running one hundred, two hundred, four hundred meters with your eyes closed. You will probably think it is impossible, but this is exactly what Ádria Rocha dos Santos does best.

Ádria was born on August 11, 1974, lived 20 years with only 10% of her vision, then she stopped seeing completely.

The skinny girl from Nanuque, Minas Gerais, is the youngest child of a large family. She has seven brothers and sisters. She decided she wanted to be an athlete when she was very young. At 13 she started to practice at the Military Police Academy of Belo Horizonte.

In 1988, at the age of 14, she participated in her first Paralympic Games in Seoul. That was the beginning of a very successful sports career.

She moved to Rio de Janeiro where she met her guide, Jorge Luiz de Souza, also known as Chocolate. She trained five to six hours daily from Monday to Saturday.

In the 1996 Paralympic Games in Atlanta, Ádria won three silver medals in the 100, 200, and 400 meters.

In Sydney, 2000, Ádria won a gold medal in the 100 meters and two silver medals in the 200 and 400 meters.

The Paralympic Games in Athens, 2004, were very important for Ádria. She won gold medals in the 100 meters and in the 200 meters. She also established a world record in the 200 meters.

Ádria lives with her daughter, Barbara, in the city of Joinville, Santa Catarina. She keeps training hard so she can perform well in every competition. She hopes that one day all paralympic athletes get the respect they deserve.

Biography 37

Based on: <http://esporte.uol.com.br>. Accessed on: April 30, 2012.

3 Check the correct alternative.

1 The text could be published in:

a ☐ a magazine. b ☐ a newspaper. c ☐ both.

2 The name of the magazine is:

a ☐ *Computer Today*. b ☐ *Sports Illustrated*. c ☐ *Biography*.

3 Ádria Rocha dos Santos was born in:

a ☐ Atlanta. b ☐ Minas Gerais. c ☐ Santa Catarina.

4 Her first participation in Paralympic Games was in:

a ☐ Sydney. b ☐ Athens. c ☐ Seoul.

4 Write T (true) or F (false).

1 ☐ The text does not mention the Barcelona Paralympic Games.

2 ☐ Ádria was born blind.

3 ☐ Ádria was born in a large family.

4 ☐ According to the text, Ádria lived in five different cities.

5 Read the text again on page 28. Answer the questions below.

1 What is Chocolate's real name?

____

2 When did Ádria start her running training?

____

6 Let's learn about some words in the text.

1 The word *picture* has several meanings. What is a synonym for it in the first sentence?

a ☐ photograph b ☐ imagine c ☐ painting

2 The sentence "... she stopped seeing completely." means:

a ☐ She got blind. b ☐ She can still see. c ☐ It was dark.

3 Find a synonym in the text for the following words:

a thin: __________ b start: __________

Let's Talk about It

As pessoas com necessidades especiais muitas vezes são negligenciadas pelos governantes. Como elas são tratadas em sua cidade? Sua cidade está preparada para atendê-las? O que você acha que poderia ser feito para que a qualidade de vida dessas pessoas melhorasse?

7 Look at the pictures and practice the conversations with a classmate. Use the verbs in the box.

play – played (2x)   prepare – prepared   study – studied
wash – washed   watch – watched

1

A: What did he do yesterday?

B: *He played the guitar yesterday.*

2

A: What did she watch last night?

B: ______________________

3

A: What did he wash this morning?

B: ______________________

4

A: What did they play yesterday?

B: ______________________

5

A: What did she study last night?

B: ______________________

6

A: What did he prepare for dinner last night?

B: ______________________

8 Write sentences about exercise 7.

1 *The boy played the guitar yesterday.*

2 ______________________

3 ______________________

4 ______________________

5 ______________________

6 ______________________

9 Talk to a classmate. Use the cues given.

1

cook lunch / last week

A: *Did he cook lunch last week?*

B: *Yes, he did.*

2

walk in the park / this afternoon

A: *Did she walk in the park this afternoon?*

B: *No, she didn't.*

3

paint the wall / yesterday

4

do her homework / this morning

5

open the window / one hour ago

6

play baseball / yesterday

12

10 Listen to the conversation. Check the correct alternative.

1 How many people are there in this conversation?

a ☐ Two. b ☐ Three. c ☐ Four.

2 They are:

a ☐ one man, two boys and one woman.

b ☐ one man, one boy, one girl and one woman.

c ☐ one man, two girls and one woman.

13

11 Listen to the conversation again and write T (true) or F (false).

1 ☐ The conversation takes place in a house.

2 ☐ The boy used the radio.

3 ☐ The girl didn't break the radio.

4 ☐ The mother used the radio.

5 ☐ The mother dropped the radio on the floor.

GRAMMAR

Simple Past – Regular Verbs

verbo + *-d* / *-ed* / *-ied*
work – work**ed**
like – like**d**
play – play**ed**
study – stud**ied**

I walk**ed**
You walk**ed**
He walk**ed**
She walk**ed**
It walk**ed**
We walk**ed**
You walk**ed**
They walk**ed**

Affirmative: She **walked** to school yesterday.
Negative: She **did not walk** to school yesterday. (did not → **didn't**)
Interrogative: **Did** she **walk** to school yesterday?
Short answers: Yes, she **did**. / No, she **didn't**.

12 Complete the sentences with the verbs in the box.

arrived | cleaned | jumped | played | watched | watered

1 Peter and Gabriel ______________ in the park yesterday.
2 They ______________ their room two hours ago.
3 The boy ______________ into the pool.
4 I ______________ the garden yesterday.
5 Vivian ______________ late last night.
6 The girls ______________ a movie yesterday.

13 Unscramble the words to form sentences.

1 watch / last night / He / TV / didn't / .
____
2 learned / verbs / new / yesterday / We / .
____
3 girl / to / talk / her / two / ago / hours / Did / the / friend / ?
____
4 dad / My / car / his / morning / this / washed / .
____
5 didn't / all / long / They / dance / night / .
____
6 visit / you / weekend / grandparents / your / last / Did / ?
____

GRAMMAR

Simple Past

O *Simple Past* refere-se a uma ação ou situação que já aconteceu.
She **arrived** late last night.

É geralmente usado com palavras que indicam tempo passado: *yesterday, last, ago, in,* entre outros.

Simple Past with Question Words

What did you **study** yesterday?	I **studied** English.
When did you **study** English?	I **studied** English yesterday.
Why did you **study** English yesterday?	I **studied** English because there was a test.

14 Rewrite the sentences in the Simple Past. Use the adverbs given.

1 My parents are watching TV now. (last night)

____

2 My mother is painting the door now. (two days ago)

____

3 He doesn't work every day. (last Saturday)

____

4 I visit my friends every year. (last year)

____

5 They aren't walking to the mall. (last night)

____

6 Martha is going to finish her lunch. (five minutes ago)

____

15 Complete the dialogue below. Use the verbs in the box in the Simple Past.

be	dance	do (2x)	enjoy	visit	walk	watch

George: What __________ you __________ on your vacation?

Lindsay: I __________ my relatives at the beach.

George: Really? What __________ you __________ there?

Lindsay: In the morning I __________ along the beach, in the afternoon I __________ the sunset and at night I __________ in a dance club.

George: __________ you __________ your trip?

Lindsay: Yes, I did. It __________ great!

16 Follow the instructions below. Work with a classmate.

Make a list of Paralympic sports.

- Choose one sport.
- Work with a classmate and do some research on the sport in magazines, newspapers, encyclopedias, the internet or interviewing people.
- Write a short article with text and pictures about that sport in the Paralympic Games.
- The class will prepare a magazine with all the articles. The magazine will be sent to the school library.

Research Notes

FUN

17 Complete the sentences with verbs in the Simple Past. Find out what Dad did last night.

1 We __________ Grandma's birthday in a restaurant.

2 Our room was dirty, so we __________ it.

3 My neighbor __________ the movie very much.

4 When the bus __________ at the bus stop, there were only a few people in line.

5 Charlie __________ a lot for his Math test.

6 My cousin __________ his bedroom last summer.

7 Columbus __________ America in 1492.

8 I was tired last night. I __________ home.

9 Frank didn't go to the office yesterday. He __________ at home.

10 Who __________ the telephone? Graham Bell.

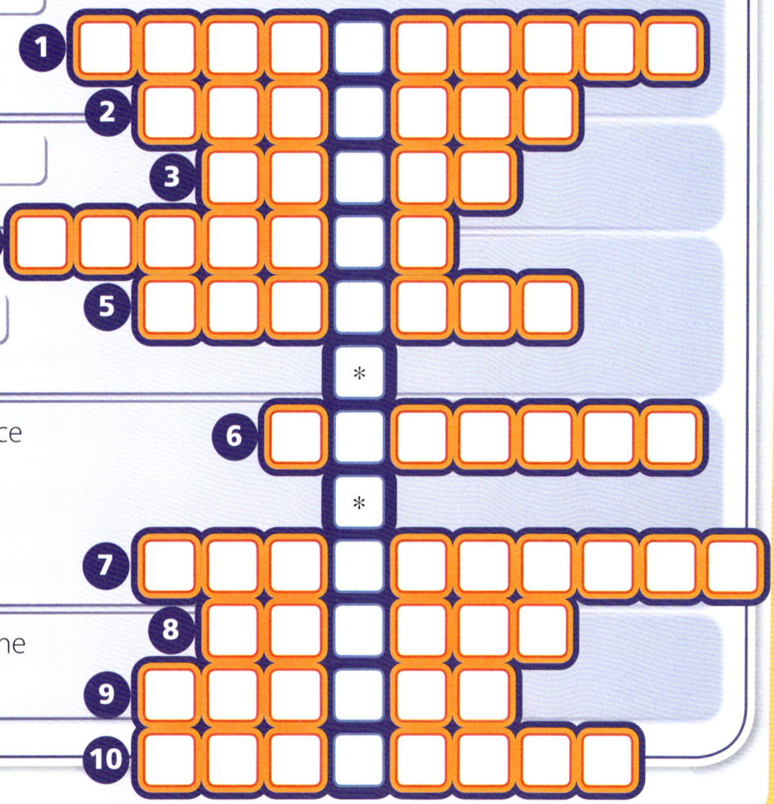

Key Language

also	established	hard	seeing	trained
best	exactly	medals	silver	vision
closed	gold	picture	skinny	won
completely	guide	probably	successful	young

Way to Go

1 Write the verbs below in the correct column to form the Simple Past.

arrive cry dance enjoy paint play prepare study use walk water work

-D	-ED	-IED

2 Use some of the verbs from exercise 1 to complete the dialogues below.

1 A: Why are you so tired, Mirelle?
B: Because yesterday I ________________ all the walls of my bedroom.
A: ________________ you ________________ your brother's too?
B: No, I ________________. Are you kidding me?

2 A: Hey, Christian. ________________ you ________________ at Gina's Real State office last year?
B: Yes. I ________________ there as a sales manager. I ________________ so much working there, but my brother ________________ from Spain and now we have our own business.
A: Great news!

3 Turn the sentences below into the Simple Past. Use the cues given.

1 The Lawsons are traveling to Rome now. (yesterday)

____

2 We don't wash the car every Saturday morning. (two days ago)

____

3 Do you call your grandparents every week? (last week)

____

4 Does Mike surf the net every afternoon? (the day before yesterday)

____

5 My sisters are watching The Grammy Awards now. (last month)

____

4 Read the dictionary entry. Then, complete the quotations below. Use the verbs from the box.

quotation
quo.ta.tion
n **1** cotação, citação, oferta. **2** orçamento para a realização de um serviço.

Extracted from: <http://michaelis.uol.com.br>. Accessed on: May 30, 2012.

founded (2x) learned stretched was

"A mind that is ______________ by a new experience can never go back to its old dimensions."
Oliver Wendell Holmes, Jr.

"All that I know I ______________ after I ______________ thirty."
Georges Clemenceau

"A friendship ______________ on business is better than a business ______________ on friendship."
John D. Rockefeller

5 Read the dictionary entry in exercise 4 again. Answer the question below.

What is the appropriate definition in Portuguese for the sentences in exercise 4?

____

6 Check the characteristics of the quotations in exercise 4.

a ☐ Long sentences.
b ☐ They were written for a specific person.
c ☐ They are easy to memorize.
d ☐ Short sentences.
e ☐ There are no authors.

7 Now it's your turn. Write your own quotation.

____
____
____

4 We Went to Brasília

1 Look at the text and answer the questions.

1 What kind of text is this?

2 Who wrote it ?

15 **2** Read the letter from Martin to his friend Liz.

Dear Liz,

We got to Brasília last Friday. The trip was very long and tiring. From the plane we saw that the city really has the shape of an airplane. Awesome!

The next morning we took a city tour. We visited the Congress building, the Cathedral and the Presidential Palace. In the afternoon we went to the TV Tower and the National Theater. Brasília looks futuristic with its unique architecture. Mike was speechless at the sight of the Cathedral.

In the evening our Brazilian friends took us to a big rock concert at the Esplanada dos Ministérios. A local band called Legion Freaks played some nice songs by Renato Russo, a famous Brazilian songwriter. I liked the songs, especially the one in Italian. My Portuguese is bad, but my Italian is OK, so I understood a little bit.

I slept all morning today because I was really tired. Mike didn't get up until 12:30 p.m. We had a quick breakfast and went to the City Park. I didn't know it's one of the largest urban parks in Brazil. It's interesting because there are trees from every part of the country.

It's almost 6 p.m. now and we're back at our hotel. Our Brazilian friends are going to take us to Pontão do Lago Sul tonight. They say it's the best place to be after the sun goes down. Let's wait and see.

Tomorrow morning we're going to the University of Brasília and finally talk to Professor Meira. He promised to help us with our project. We're going to spend the whole day at the university. In the evening we're going to visit some friends.

Our flight to Manaus is on Tuesday morning.

I'll write more about our trip when we get there.

I think of you all the time. Hope you are getting better.

Love,

Martin

3 Write T (true) or F (false).

1 [ ] Liz is probably sick.
2 [ ] Renato Russo didn't sing in the concert.
3 [ ] It is possible to infer that Martin is a university student.
4 [ ] It is possible to infer that Martin doesn't know Professor Meira.

4 Answer the questions below.

1 Does Martin live in Brasília?

____

2 Who did Martin and Mike go to the rock concert with?

____

3 Did Martin understand the songs in Portuguese?

____

5 Complete the travel plan according to the text.

TRAVEL PLAN	
Place	Brasília
Date of arrival	Friday, 17th
Arrival time	9:00 p.m. – Brasília International Airport
Day 1	
Morning	
Afternoon	
Evening	
Day 2	
Morning	Free time at the hotel
Afternoon	
Evening	
Day 3	
Morning	Fly to Manaus

Let's Talk about It

Um dos maiores prazeres da vida, na opinião de muitas pessoas, é viajar. Você concorda? Justifique sua resposta. Quais lugares você gostaria de conhecer? Por quê?

GRAMMAR

Simple Past – Irregular Verbs

Os verbos irregulares têm uma forma própria para o passado; eles não seguem regras. Quando o verbo auxiliar *did* aparece na frase, o verbo principal fica no infinitivo sem *to*.

Affirmative: She **bought** her book two days ago.
Interrogative: **Did** she **buy** her book two days ago?
Negative: She **did not buy** her book two days ago.

didn't (= did not)

Short answers: Yes, she **did**.
No, she **didn't**.

What did he **sell**?
Where did you **buy** your jacket?
When did she **give** you the money?
Who did you **think** about?
How much did the book **cost**?
How many books **did** you **buy**?

6 Write sentences. Use the cues given.

1 Amanda / to bring sandwiches / yesterday / .
Amanda brought sandwiches yesterday.

2 David / to get up / two hours ago / .
______

3 Robert / not to sleep in his room / this morning / .
______

4 Judith / to sell her bicycle / last week / .
______

5 Nicholas / not to eat pasta / last night / .
______

7 Answer the questions. Use the words given.

1 How much did this picture cost? (US$98)
______

2 What did you bring to the party? (candy)
______

3 Where did she put the maps? (drawer)
______

4 When did they buy the presents? (the day before yesterday)
______

5 How many books did you read last year?
______

8 Do some research on the internet or in books. Answer the questions below.

1 Brasília has the shape of an airplane. Who created the concept of the city?

____

2 What was his occupation?

____

3 The Presidential Palace, the Cathedral and all the main public buildings of Brasília have impressive, modern architecture. Who designed all those buildings?

____

4 How old was that famous architect when he designed all those buildings?

____

5 On April 22, 1960, Brasília was formally declared Brazil's national capital. Who was the President at that time?

____

6 How long was he the President of Brazil?

____

9 Look at the pictures and practice the conversations with a classmate.

1

Steve / drink / a glass of orange juice / a glass of milk

A: *What did Steve drink yesterday?*
B: *He drank a glass of orange juice.*
A: *Did he drink a glass of orange juice last week, too?*
B: *No, he didn't. He drank a glass of milk.*

2

Vivian / drive / car / bus

3

the man / ride / motorcycle / bike

4

the children / eat / spaghetti / pizza

5

you / write / letter / note

10 Look at the pictures in exercise 9. Underline the correct words.

1 Steve drank orange juice **yesterday** / **last week**.

2 Vivian **drove** / **didn't drive** a bus yesterday.

3 The man rode a **motorcycle** / **bicycle** yesterday.

4 The children **ate** / **didn't eat** spaghetti last week.

5 You **wrote** / **didn't write** a note last week.

16 **11** Listen to the dialogue. Check the correct alternative.

1 How many people participate in this conversation?

a ☐ One.

b ☐ Two.

c ☐ Three.

2 The people involved in the conversation are:

a ☐ all Brazilians.

b ☐ a tour guide and the tourists.

c ☐ all tourists.

3 The President works at:

a ☐ the Supreme Court.

b ☐ the Congress building.

c ☐ the Planalto Palace.

4 The two big towers are:

a ☐ office buildings.

b ☐ the President's office.

c ☐ the Supreme Court.

12 Listen to the conversation again. Write the names of the buildings.

____

____

____

____

____

____

____

13 Read the postcard below. Then write one about your last trip. Follow the steps given.

- Where and how you went.
- What you did there.
- Who went with you.
- If you liked the trip and why.

Dear uncle Jeff,
You were right! Brasília is really impressive! So modern and exciting. The food is great and the hotel is fantastic. The buildings here look like works of art. Yesterday we went to Brasília Cathedral. It's awesome! We bought you a souvenir.
Miss you.
Jim and Anna

Brasília
January 8th, 2013

Jefferson Barthes
15th East Street, 31
New York NY 10073
U.S.

FUN

14 Find 12 verbs in the Simple Past.

F	K	Y	D	M	W	L	V	E	S	Q	L	O	C	O	S	T	D
L	I	U	I	B	V	R	F	D	W	L	K	G	Y	U	N	B	F
J	S	L	D	Q	Z	I	U	N	B	R	F	D	A	I	Y	R	G
B	A	C	D	L	D	R	A	N	K	Y	S	D	T	V	H	O	M
N	T	A	P	L	M	Y	H	G	D	K	O	V	E	C	S	U	N
K	U	H	T	B	N	M	P	O	F	K	L	Q	S	F	Z	G	Q
B	W	E	N	T	M	L	K	G	E	E	D	S	W	Q	X	H	M
P	Y	H	J	K	F	E	R	T	L	V	F	A	Q	C	D	T	S
A	Z	E	Y	U	I	L	P	O	L	H	N	T	G	R	W	D	S
Q	X	B	G	I	K	J	B	O	U	G	H	T	R	D	W	S	P
L	G	A	V	E	A	Z	C	D	E	R	N	H	G	C	U	T	K

3 letters

4 letters

5 letters

6 letters

7 letters

17 **Key Language**

a little bit awesome get better songwriter whole day

Way to Go

1 Complete the verb chart below.

INFINITIVE	SIMPLE PAST	TRANSLATION
buy		comprar
	went	ir
see	saw	
get up		levantar-se
	brought	trazer
sing		
	sold	
	cost	

2 Complete the dialogue between Mark and Jim. Use the verbs in the box in the Simple Past.

bring (2x) buy (2x) come go (3x) order (2x)

Mark: Hey, dude!

Jim: What's up, Mark?

Mark: ____________ you ____________ to Mamma's Bakery yesterday?

Jim: Yes, I ____________ there at 4 a.m. yesterday. You know, Danielle's surprise birthday party is next Friday.

Mark: That's why I'm worried. ____________ you ____________ the cake?

Jim: Sure, I did. I ____________ a wonderful cake and some sausage rolls. I also ____________ to the All for Parties Shop the day before yesterday.

Mark: Really? What ____________ you ____________ there?

Jim: Well, I ____________ some balloons, a new table cloth and napkins.

Mark: Fine!

Jim: Guess who ____________ over to my place this morning and ____________ some stuff for the party?

Mark: Marcie?

Jim: Yes! She ____________ some bottles of soda!

Mark: No kidding! She hates spending money!

Jim: That's surprising, isn't it?

3 Read the dialogue in exercise 2 again. Answer the questions below.

1 Did Jim go with Mark to Mamma's Bakery?

____

2 What time did Jim go to Mamma's Bakery?

____

3 Where else did Jim go yesterday?

____

4 What did he buy there?

____

5 What did Marcie bring to Jim's place?

____

4 Order the sentences to form a paragraph about Amelia Earhart.

Amelia Earhart

( ) In 1937, she mysteriously disappeared while trying to circumnavigate the globe on the Equator.

( ) On May 15, 1923, Amelia Earhart became the 16th woman to be issued a pilot's license.

(1) Aviator Amelia Earhart was born on July 24, 1897, in Atchison, Kansas.

( ) She had several notable flights and became the first woman to fly across the Atlantic in 1928.

Extracted from: <www.biography.com>.
Accessed on: May 7, 2012.

5 Read the paragraph about Amelia Earhart again. Write T (true) or F (false).

1 [ ] Amelia Earhart was forty when she disappeared.

2 [ ] She was British.

3 [ ] Amelia Earhart didn't have a license to fly airplanes.

4 [ ] She crossed the Atlantic at the age of 31.

5 In the Media

1 Look at the texts and answer.

1 What kind of texts are these?

2 What are these sentences used for?

18 **2** Read the headlines below.

① Hero dog saves boy, 11, from cougar attack

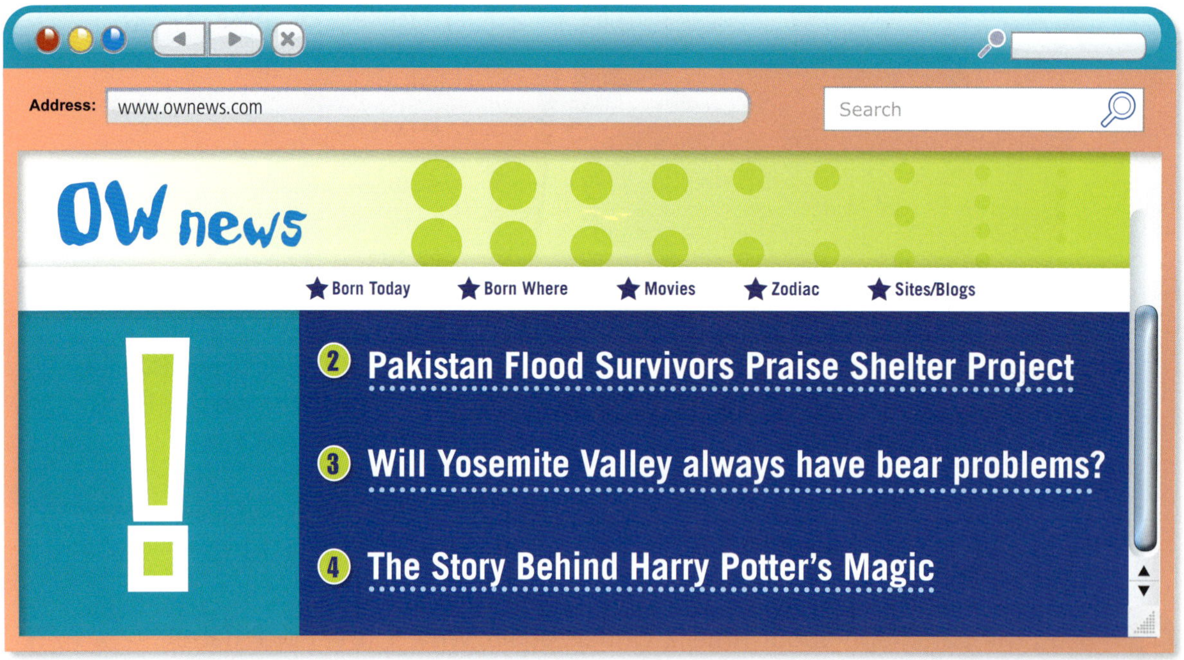
Address: www.ownews.com

Search

OW news

★ Born Today ★ Born Where ★ Movies ★ Zodiac ★ Sites/Blogs

② Pakistan Flood Survivors Praise Shelter Project

③ Will Yosemite Valley always have bear problems?

④ The Story Behind Harry Potter's Magic

3 Number the sentences according to the headlines above.

- [ ] How everything started.
- [ ] The boy escaped the attack.
- [ ] Bears steal food from picnic baskets.
- [ ] Not everybody was killed in the flood.

4. Read the extracts below. Match them to the corresponding headlines in exercise 2 on page 48.

( ) ______________________________

[...]
"I was milking a cow when I heard about the flood," says Balaneeshta, a woman living in northern Pakistan. "People from far away were saying 'run!'" Balaneeshta and her neighbors ran up the mountains to safety. With homes completely washed away, villagers slept outside for days.
[...]

Adapted from: <http://crs-blog.org>. Accessed on: May 9, 2012.

( ) ______________________________

[...]
J.K. Rowling has said that Harry Potter jumped into her mind during a train ride, and that the story followed suit, but the truth is that Harry Potter and his world came from a deep connection with her childhood and the experiences that took place in her early life. [...]

Extracted from: <http://escholarship.bc.edu588>. Accessed on: May 9, 2012.

( ) ______________________________

[...]
Yosemite Valley is the main attraction in Yosemite National Park... not only for people, but also for bears, and the presence of people's food makes it all that more attractive to bears.
[...]

Extracted from: <http://jeffreytrust.wordpress.com>. Accessed on: May 9, 2012.

( ) ______________________________

By Mike Celizic

TODAY.com contributor

The 11-year-old boy didn't have time to react — and barely enough time to realize that a cougar was flying toward him with dinner on its mind. Luckily for Austin Forman, his dog, Angel, threw herself between her best friend and a lethal predator.
[...]

Extracted from: <http://today.msnbc.msn.com>. Accessed on: May 9, 2012.

Let's Talk about It

Algumas manchetes apresentam certo exagero na escolha das palavras. Por que você acha que isso acontece? Você já se sentiu frustrado após ler uma notícia e perceber que o conteúdo não refletiu o que a manchete sugeria?

5 Practice the conversations with a classmate.

1

Chris and Alex

2

Anna and Lynn

3

Alice and Ray

A: *What were Chris and Alex doing when you arrived?*

B: *They were playing the guitar.*

4

the painter

5

the kids

6

Evelyn

6 Write sentences about the people in exercise 5.

Anna and Lynn *They were eating sandwiches.*

Alice and Ray

___

the painter

___

the kids

___

Evelyn

___

GRAMMAR

Past Continuous

I **was** work**ing**
You **were** work**ing**
He / She / It — **was** work**ing**
We / You / They — **were** work**ing**

Affirmative: He **was** work**ing**.
Negative: He **was not** work**ing**.
Interrogative: **Was** he work**ing**?
Short answer: Yes, he **was**. / No, he **wasn't**.

O *Past Continuous* descreve uma ação em andamento no passado. Esse tempo verbal é muito usado em narrativas.

7 Complete the sentences with the Past Continuous. Use the verbs from the box.

fish paint play study (neg.) wear work (neg.)

1 She *wasn't studying* Geography. She was watching TV.
2 Paul ______________ the wall yesterday morning.
3 ______________ they ______________ tennis at the tennis court?
4 I ______________ my best dress at the party.
5 ______________ she ______________ in a lake?
6 They ______________ in their office. They were having dinner at home.

8 Answer the questions.

1 What was the girl doing when the children arrived? (sing)
She was singing.
2 What were you doing when the fire started? (watch TV)
____
3 What was he doing when he saw her? (cross the street)
____
4 What were they doing when the accident happened? (sleep)
____
5 What was he doing when the cougar attacked? (walk in the forest)
____
6 What was he doing when his girlfriend called him? (take a shower)
____

9 Listen and number the pictures in the correct sequence.

10 Write a sentence about each picture.

1 *Austin and his dog went out to bring in some wood.*

2 ______________________________

3 ______________________________

4 ______________________________

5 ______________________________

6 ______________________________

GRAMMAR

Past Continuous

O *Past Continuous* pode aparecer sozinho ou em conjunto com o *Simple Past*, acompanhados dos advérbios *when* (quando), *while* (enquanto), *yesterday*, *ago*, *last*, etc.

I was studying **when** you arrived.
Harry was sleeping **while** his sister was studying.
They were working one hour **ago**.

11 Complete the sentences with the Simple Past or the Past Continuous. Use the verbs in parentheses.

1 Mike *was talking* (talk) to his boss when I saw him.

2 My sister and I ________________ (watch) a movie on TV when our cousin came in.

3 Where ________________ they ________________ (go) to when they hit a bicycle?

4 What were you doing when the door bell ________________ (ring)?

5 ________________ she ________________ (have) dinner when her boyfriend ________________ (arrive)?

6 While I ________________ (talk) on the phone, my brother ________________ (clean) the room.

7 When they left the office, it ________________ (rain) a lot.

8 The girls ________________ (swim) while the boys ________________ (play) soccer.

12 Answer the questions about yourself. Use short answers.

1 Were you studying Geography an hour ago?

____

2 Were you reading when the teacher arrived?

____

3 Were your classmates studying when you entered the classroom?

____

4 Was a classmate talking while the teacher was speaking last class?

____

5 Was it raining when you got up this morning?

____

6 Was the teacher explaining Math 5 minutes ago?

____

13 Write appropriate sentences under each headline. Use the information from the boxes A and B.

A

- The Titanic was crossing the Atlantic
- A woman was watching fireworks
- A famous singer was performing in England
- A housewife was watering the garden
- A man was swimming

B

- when a shark attacked him.
- when a dog bit her.
- when it hit an iceberg and sank.
- when she saw a UFO.
- when he fell off the stage and broke his leg.

Titanic hits an iceberg and sinks

The Titanic was crossing the Atlantic when it hit an iceberg and sank.

Housewife sees UFO in her garden

Justin Bieber breaks his leg

Dog bites woman watching fireworks

Shark attacks swimmer

FUN

14 Use the letters below to form words.

E	R	E	E
B	A	S	U
D	N	W	C
G	I	O	L
A	K	G	O
T	H	C	B

Key Language

20

behind	fish	home	people	see
clean	flood	jump	play	survivor
cross	go	mountains	run	talk
fall	have	neighbors	save	watch
find	hear	paint	say	wear

Way to Go

1 Write meaningful sentences. Use expressions from the boxes.

The teachers were watching the ceremony Jeremy was studying in Paris I was studying Math Jessica was cleaning her room	when (2x) while (2x)	his parents were working hard in Dallas to support him. Jonathan was cleaning his. I noticed my calculator wasn't on my desk. the students came in and surprised them with flowers.

The teachers were watching the ceremony when the students came in and surprised them with flowers.

____

____

____

2 Write questions and answers. Use the cues given.

1

What / Jane / do / when / Marcus / arrive / at the party?

What was Jane doing when Marcus arrived at the party?
She was taking pictures.

2

What / the kids / do / while / their mother / look for them?

____

____

3

What / Tommy / do / when / meet / Joseph?

____

____

4

Who / Mary Ann / talking to / when / the cell phone / ring?

____

____

3 Read the text below. Complete it with verbs from the box in the Simple Past or in the Past Continuous.

be cry give go leave notice run see talk turn

From: lucy@ow.com
To: sally@ow.com

Send Attach

Hi, Sally

Yesterday afternoon I ______________ to a nice coffee house with a friend of mine, Janet. We ______________ and laughing when Janet ______________ her husband walking calmly down the street with a very beautiful blonde woman. Janet ______________ very surprised and angry. Suddenly, her husband ______________ the woman a hug and a tender kiss on her cheek! Janet ______________ the coffee house immediately, running towards them. She ______________ and screaming. She grabbed her husband's shoulder and, when he ______________ to her, she noticed it wasn't Jason! The blonde woman was afraid of the crazy lady and the man was speechless! At the same time, the waiter from the coffee house ______________ after us because the check wasn't paid!

Oh, my… what a shame!

XOXO

Lucy

4 Read the text in exercise 3 again. Answer the questions below.

1 Where were the two friends yesterday afternoon?

____

2 What were they doing?

____

3 What was Janet's first reaction when she saw the man with the blonde woman?

____

5 What can we infer about Janet?

a ☐ She is an extroverted person.

b ☐ She is a jealous person.

c ☐ She is very unhappy.

6 Healthy Salad

1 Take a look at the page and answer.

1 What are the main ingredients in the recipe below?

2 Do you know any recipe by heart?

21 **2** Read the text below.

Lettuce Boats

Here's what you will need to make them:

- large lettuce leaves
- your favorite salad veggies like chopped carrots, cucumbers, tomatoes, and red peppers
- croutons
- your favorite salad dressing

Here's what you have to do:

1 Check with a grown-up before you start this.

2 First you need to wash and dry your lettuce really well.

3 Take your lettuce leaf and drizzle some of your favorite salad dressing down the middle.

4 Now sprinkle on some of your favorite chopped veggies like carrots, cucumbers, tomatoes, red peppers – whatever you like!

5 Add a few croutons.

6 Fold the lettuce leaf.

7 Now your lettuce boat is ready to eat. It can be a little messy so you might want to eat it over a plate.

Adapted from: <http://pbskids.org>. Accessed on: May 9, 2012.

3 Read the text on page 58 again. Check the appropriate alternatives.

1 What are the main meals of the day?
- a [ ] Coffee, lunch and supper.
- b [ ] Breakfast, snack and dinner.
- c [ ] Breakfast, lunch and dinner.

2 The text is:
- a [ ] Poetic.
- b [ ] Narrative.
- c [ ] Instructional.

3 How many steps are necessary to make the Lettuce Boat?
- a [ ] Ten. b [ ] Seven. c [ ] Nine.

4 What are croutons?
- a [ ] Small pieces of toasted bread.
- b [ ] A kind of cookie.
- c [ ] A kind of juice.

4 Match the columns.

1 drizzle	a [ ]	let a little quantity of a liquid fall over some food.
2 add	b [ ]	put together one side of something to its opposite side.
3 fold	c [ ]	join to something else.

5 Answer the questions below.

1 Which are the veggies mentioned in the recipe?

____

2 Why is it appropriate to eat the Lettuce Boat over a plate?

____

3 What sentence confirms that you should talk to an adult before making the Lettuce Boat?

____

Let's Talk about It

Atualmente as famílias dividem as tarefas domésticas para não sobrecarregar apenas uma pessoa. Você costuma ajudar nas tarefas domésticas? Se sim, o que costuma fazer? Se não, por quê?

6 Practice the conversations. Use the cues given.

1 beautiful woman

A: *Who is the most beautiful woman in your opinion?*

B: *It's Gisele Bündchen.*

A: *I think Gloria Stefan is more beautiful than Gisele.*

B: *I agree. / I don't agree.*

2 dangerous animal

A: *What is the most dangerous animal in your opinion?*

B: *It's the lion.*

A: *I think the elephant is more dangerous than the lion.*

B: *Really? / I don't think so.*

3 interesting movie

4 handsome man

5 delicious cake

6 expensive car

7 difficult subject

8 delicious food

7 Write about them.

1

Angelina Jolie

Jennifer Aniston

1 attractive

Jennifer Aniston is more attractive than Angelina Jolie. / Angelina Jolie is more attractive than Jennifer Aniston.

2

rapel

rafting

2 dangerous

____

____

____

3

Johnny Depp

Leonardo DiCaprio

3 talented

____

____

____

GRAMMAR

Degrees of Comparison

More… than (mais… que) é usado com adjetivos de duas ou mais sílabas.
I am **more** intelligent **than** my brother.

The most… (o mais) é usado com adjetivos de duas ou mais sílabas.
Alice is **the most** intelligent person in class.

Less… than (menos… que) é usado com adjetivos de uma ou mais sílabas.
A cat is **less** dangerous **than** a lion.

The least… (o menos…) é usado com adjetivos de uma ou mais sílabas.
This is **the least** expensive dress I have.

8 Complete the sentences below. Use the adjectives in the box.

comfortable economical energetic expensive obedient talented

1 Kids are *more energetic than* adults.
2 The living room is ______________ place in this house.
3 In your opinion, who is ______________ actor in Brazil?
4 Dogs are ______________ cats.
5 A trip by ship is ______________ a trip by plane.
6 Modern cars are ______________ those from the 1990's.

9 Answer the questions. Give true answers about yourself.

1 What subject is less difficult than English?
____
2 What subject is more difficult than English?
____
3 What is the least difficult subject for you?
____
4 What is the most expensive car you know?
____
5 What is less dangerous than parachuting?
____
6 What is [illegible] eautiful city you know?
____

GRAMMAR

Tag Questions

Tag Questions são perguntas feitas para confirmar algo dito ou para pedir uma informação. São formadas por um verbo auxiliar e um pronome sempre ao final das frases.

Oração afirmativa ⟶ ***Tag Question* negativa**
Mary is studying, **isn't she**?
You work every day, **don't you**?
Sally sings well, **doesn't she**?
They studied hard, **didn't they**?
We can swim, **can't we**?

Oração negativa ⟶ ***Tag Question* afirmativa**
Mary isn't studying now, **is she**?
You don't work every day, **do you**?
Sally doesn't sing well, **does she**?
They didn't study hard, **did they**?
We can't swim, **can we**?

Casos especiais:
I'm too thin for that dress, **aren't I**?
Sit down, **will you**?

10 Match the sentences to the correct Tag Question.

1 Peter isn't going shopping,
2 The children were playing in the pool,
3 I'm getting fat,
4 That girl started a new English course,
5 Daniela can speak two languages,
6 The boys don't live near the gas station,
7 My cousin wasn't absent last class,
8 That little boy was sick,
9 We work eight hours a day,

a [ ] wasn't he?
b [ ] can't she?
c [ ] was she?
d [*1*] is he?
e [ ] don't we?
f [ ] weren't they?
g [ ] aren't I?
h [ ] do they?
i [ ] didn't she?

11 Complete the sentences. Use Tag Questions.

1 Dad is talking on his phone, *isn't he*?
2 You like bread and butter, ______________?
3 We can go out tonight, ______________?
4 The Bakers sent us many postcards, ______________?
5 Jane likes cooking lunch, ______________?

12 Complete the sentences with the prepositions *in*, *on*, *at*, *under*, *after*, *before*.

1 The oranges are __________ the box.
2 We don't go to school __________ the morning.
3 She goes to work __________ 7 a.m.
4 June comes __________ May.
5 The presents are __________ the Christmas tree.
6 Your dress is __________ the bed.
7 He has English classes __________ Mondays.
8 I'm cooking a delicious fish. Come home __________ dinner!

13 Practice the conversations with your classmate.

1

they / happy

A: *They are happy, aren't they?*
B: *I think so. / Not really.*

2

Ray / buy / a car

3

she / sleep

4

they / play / soccer

5

they / like / ice cream

6

he/ like / salad

22 **14** Listen to the dialogues. Write C (correct) or W (wrong).

1 ☐ 4 ☐ 7 ☐
2 ☐ 5 ☐ 8 ☐
3 ☐ 6 ☐ 9 ☐

15 You have to create and write a delicious dessert recipe. Follow the steps below.

- Use some of the ingredients listed. You can use all of them if you want.
- Use the verbs and the vocabulary given.
- Don't forget to name your dessert.
- Organize your recipe like this: title, ingredients and directions.

- 1 can of sliced peaches
- 1 pack of chocolate cookies
- Cinnamon
- Vanilla ice cream
- 1 can of condensed milk
- Juice of 3 lemons

- Sprinkle
- Mix
- Add
- Spread
- Crush
- Put

- Spoon
- Bowl
- Dessert bowl

FUN

16 Play the sentence bingo.

1 NOUNS

a book, a cat, a chair, a dictionary, a dog, a sofa, baseball, buses, cake, cats, DiCaprio, dogs, Gisele, ice cream, Johnny Depp, lions, Luisa, planes, rhinos, ships, soccer, trains

2 VERBS

are, aren't, is, isn't

3 ADJECTIVES

beautiful, charming, comfortable, dangerous, delicious, economical, elegant, expensive, handsome, interesting, obedient

BINGO CHART

	1 NOUN	2 VERB	3 ADJECTIVE	1 NOUN
1	*Ships*	*are*	more *charming* than	*planes.*
2			more than	
3			more than	
4			more than	
5			more than	

23 **Key Language**

attractive	dangerous	important	most
breakfast	difficult	kitchen	popular
brush	economical	least	recipe
butter	expensive	less	veggies
cook	handsome	more	

Way to Go

1 Check the wrong sentences. Rewrite and correct them.

1 ☐ Poisonous snakes are more dangerous than eagles.

____

2 ☐ The onion soup is the most good appetizer in Jack's restaurant.

____

3 ☐ Math is less boring Geography, isn't it?

____

4 ☐ Traveling by bus is more comfortable than traveling by car.

____

5 ☐ Which cake is the least tasteful than to you?

____

2 Read the dialogue below. Write the appropriate Tag Question.

Pam: Hi, Tanya!

Tanya: Hi, Pam.

Pam: You aren't busy now, ______________?

Tanya: Not at all. What can I do for you?

Pam: I have a present to buy...

Tanya: That's true! Tomorrow is your sister's birthday, ______________?

Pam: Yeah... I really don't know what to buy for an eighteen-year-old girl. Can you help me?

Tanya: Maybe a make-up kit... oh, no! Your mother gave her one last year, ______________?

Pam: No. My mother bought her a dress. That's a great idea for a present! You and I can go to the mall together and look for a nice make-up kit, ______________?

Tanya: Sure! You don't have classes on Thursdays afternoon, ______________?

Pam: No. We can go to the mall, then.

Tanya: Deal!

3 Do you like to cook? Listen to some rules for the kitchen and fill in the gaps.

Rules for the kitchen

1 Always ______________ an adult if you can ______________ the kitchen.

2 ______________ an apron to ______________ your clothes clean.

3 ______________ your hands with soap and water before starting your preparations. Wash hands as needed like after touching the trash can or picking items up from the floor.

4 Re ______________ the recipe several times.

5 Make sure you ______________ all the ingredients you ______________ before you start. ______________ them out on the counter.

6 Put all equipment such as pans, measuring cups and measuring spoons out on the counter.

7 ______________ the recipe exactly.

8 Always ______________ up when you are finished.

Extracted from: <www.recipegoldmine.com>. Accessed on: May 12, 2012.

4 Check the appropriate alternative.

1 Most verbs in the rules are in the:

a ☐ imperative form.

b ☐ present form.

c ☐ past form.

2 The items related to hygienic habits are:

a ☐ 3 and 4.

b ☐ 6 and 8.

c ☐ 3 and 8.

3 Why is rule number 1 so important? Answer in Portuguese.

____

____

____

7 Man's Best Friend

1 Take a look at the text. Answer the questions below.

1 What kind of text is this?

2 Who is the target reader of this text?

25 **2** Read the text below.

Do you like them...
bigger or smaller?
With short or long hair?
Shyer or more playful?
More active or more peaceful?

There are things you should know before you decide to have a pet.

Dogs that are found on the streets go to special kennels. They wait for their owners for up to five days. After that period, the healthiest and the most docile go for adoption.

The others are sacrificed.

In São Paulo, for example, more than 50 dogs are taken from the streets every day.

Only a few of them are adopted.

Imagine what happens to the others.

Do you really want a pet?

Then answer this question first:

What kind of pet owner are you?

ADOPT ME!

Age: 8 months
Sex: male
Size: small
Name: Carrot

3 Fill in the pet adoption form. Compare your answers to a classmate's.

PET ADOPTION FORM

1 Do you really like pets?

( ) Yes. ( ) No. ( ) Sometimes.

2 Can you offer a good standard of living for your pet? (Food, vaccines, etc.)

( ) Yes. ( ) No. ( ) Not always.

3 Do you have time to wash, walk and play with your pet?

( ) Yes. ( ) No. ( ) Not always.

4 Are you patient?

( ) Yes. ( ) No. ( ) Not always.

5 Are you allergic to dogs and cats?

( ) Yes. ( ) No. ( ) Sometimes.

6 Did you know that…

- a dog may live up to 15 years?

  ( ) Yes. ( ) No. ( ) That's too much!

- dogs and cats are funny but they may do bad things? (Pee on the carpet, for example.)

  ( ) Yes. ( ) No. ( ) Not in my house.

- dogs can't live tied to one place? (Movement is necessary for their intelligence.)

  ( ) Yes. ( ) No. ( ) I don't think so.

- dogs need food at regular intervals?

  ( ) Yes. ( ) No. ( ) I don't think so.

- a pet needs love and affection?

  ( ) Yes. ( ) No. ( ) I don't think so.

Let's Talk about It

Muitas pessoas acreditam que ter um animal de estimação em casa deixa o ambiente mais alegre. Você concorda com isso? Qual é sua opinião sobre as pessoas que comercializam animais domésticos como cães e gatos? O que as autoridades podem fazer para minimizar o problema de animais abandonados nas grandes cidades?

GRAMMAR

Comparatives

Acrescenta-se a terminação *er* aos adjetivos de uma sílaba para formar o comparativo de superioridade.

er than: mais… que

Jeremy is almost 2 meters tall. He is **taller than** his father.

Acrescenta-se a terminação *est* aos adjetivos de uma sílaba para formar o superlativo.

the… est: o mais…

Jeremy is **the tallest** player in his basketball team.

Adjetivos terminados em *y* trocam o *y* por *i* e recebem a terminação *er* ou *est*.

happ**y** → happ**ier** → happ**iest**
ugl**y** → ugl**ier** → ugl**iest**

Adjetivos terminados em consoante + vogal + consoante dobram a consoante final e recebem *er* ou *est*.

big → bi**gger** → bi**ggest**
thin → thi**nner** → thi**nnest**

4 Complete the sentences below. Use the correct form of the Adjectives in the box.

cheap cute happy long short thick

1 Why is Tom ______________ today than he was yesterday?
2 Winter nights are ______________ than summer nights.
3 February is the ______________ month of the year.
4 That book is very thick. Is it the ______________ book in the library?
5 Is a hot dog ______________ than a hamburger?
6 Lucy is a cute girl. She is the ______________ girl I know.

5 Write questions and answers. Use the cues given.

1 your house / small / mine / Nick's
A: *Is your house smaller than mine?*
B: *Yes, it is. But Nick's house is the smallest.*

2 your mom / tall / your teacher / my aunt
A: ______________________
B: ______________________

3 the U.S. / big / Brazil / Canada
A: ______________________
B: ______________________

6 Write two sentences about the animals in the picture below. Use the Adjectives given.

1 tall

The giraffe is taller than the elephants.

The giraffe is the tallest of all the animals in the picture.

2 strong

____

____

3 fast

____

____

____

4 weak

____

____

____

5 short

____

____

____

____

7 Read the cartoon. Check the best alternative to complete the sentences.

1 The cat is asking a question:

a ☐ to a man who probably wants to adopt it.

b ☐ to a man who hates pets.

c ☐ to its owner.

2 The man seems to be:

a ☐ happy.

b ☐ shy.

c ☐ surprised.

26 **8** Listen to the dialogues. Look at the pictures and check the correct alternative.

1

Joanna

Angela

- [ ] Angela is taller than Joanna.
- [ ] Joanna is taller than Angela.
- [ ] Angela is as tall as Joanna.

2

Grandma

Grandpa

- [ ] Grandpa is the oldest person in the family.
- [ ] Grandpa is younger than grandma.
- [ ] Grandma is the oldest person in the family.

3

Billy

Fluffy

- [ ] Billy is fatter than Fluffy.
- [ ] Fluffy is as fat as Billy.
- [ ] Fluffy is fatter than Billy.

9 Read the dialogues below. Choose the best words to complete them.

1 peaceful peace

A: Was there any trouble at the student's protest?
B: No troubles at all. The protest was ________________.

2 happy unhappy

A: Why are you so ________________, Jane?
B: I didn't pass my entrance exam.

3 play playful

A: Liam's cats are very ________________, aren't they?
B: Yes, they really are. They are always playing with balls of wool or rubber toys.

10 Answer the questions.

1 Who is the tallest person in your family?

____

2 What is the most delicious dessert you know?

____

3 In your opinion, what is the most interesting subject in school?

____

4 Who is the funniest classmate you have?

____

11 Look at the pictures and practice the conversation with a classmate. Use the Adjectives from the box.

chetah

turtle

elephant

giraffe

bear

lion

monkey

snake

crocodile

fast	faster	the fastest
short	shorter	the shortest
slow	slower	the slowest
small	smaller	the smallest
strong	stronger	the strongest
tall	taller	the tallest
weak	weaker	the weakest

A: Which animal is taller: the elephant or the giraffe?

B: The giraffe is taller than the elephant.

A: What is the tallest animal?

B: The giraffe is the tallest.

12 Read a leaflet for an adoption campaign. Write about Shadow, the cat.

HAPPY PETS

His name is Baron. He's three years old. He gives kisses and will give you his paw to shake when asked. He is smart and sweet and is looking for the perfect home and family.

She is Star. Star is the most obedient and smartest dog in the world. She is very playful and loves children. She is two years old. She is looking for a nice home.

Shadow – 4 months old – small – sweet – affectionate

____

____

____

____

____

FUN

13 Find names of animals hidden in the sentences.

1. Open the door at once!
   rat
2. That will be a real help.
3. He came late yesterday.
4. He arrived in America today.
5. Eric owes me ten cents.
6. Do good workers succeed?
7. If I shout, he'll hear me.
8. She's sitting in the sixth or seventh row.
9. In April I only come here once.
10. I have to clean the pan daily.
11. A gold key isn't a common key.

27 **Key Language**

affectionate	owner	playful
healthiest	paw	shyer
kennel	peaceful	smart

Way to Go

1 Complete the chart below.

tall	taller than	
comfortable		the most comfortable
small	smaller than	
	more interesting than	the most interesting
happy	happier than	
		the thickest
boring	more boring than	
	shyer than	
	slower than	the slowest
fast		the fastest
	stronger than	

2 Use some of the Adjectives in exercise 1 to complete the dialogues.

1 **A:** Is your beach house ______________________ your city house?

B: Of course it is! We have four bedrooms and five bathrooms there.

2 **A:** Jonathan's car is ______________________ Mariah's, isn't it?

B: Sure. Seven people can get into it easily but not comfortably!

3 **A:** Chris said Mr. Andrew's lectures about ancient history are ______________________.

B: Why did he say that?

A: Because he wants to sleep every time he attends them.

4 **A:** I can't believe that. Dan wanted so much to meet Janice, but when he met her, he became ______________ boy in the party!

B: That was really unbelievable. He is always so extroverted! He must be in love...

5 **A:** Which book is ______________________ the Bible?

B: I don't know. How many pages are there in the Bible?

6 **A:** Is Stelle ______________________ girl in the class?

B: Yes, she is. Stelle is almost 1.90 meters tall.

3 Read the extracts below. Complete them with Adjectives from the box.

expensive	largest	longest	oldest

The record for the world's ______________________ chocolate sculpture was broken this week in Irvine, California. It weighs 18,239 pounds.

Three tourists track across 4 continents. It is the world's ______________________ taxi ride.

A version of Edvard Munch's *The Scream* was sold yesterday for an incredible $119,922,500 U.S. dollars (£74 million). It is the world's most ______________________ painting sold at auction.

Fearless Peggy McAlpine, 104, is the world's ______________________ paraglider.

Adapted from: <www.guinnessworldrecords.com>. Accessed on: May 16, 2012.

8 Skydiving

1 Look at the text and pictures and answer.

1 Do you like extreme sports?

2 Can you name some extreme air sports?

28 **2** Read the text below.

Address: http://skydivechick.com

Search

X-Sports

Sports Talk

SKYDIVERS: ARE THEY CRAZY?

Although extreme sports are considered much more dangerous than traditional sports, thousands of athletes around the world try them every day. Are they crazy? Skydiving, skysurfing, wingsurfing are some of the extreme air sports. Expert Melanie Curtis tells us about her love for skydiving.

XP: How did you start?

Melanie: I was exposed to skydiving at a young age. I could have started when I was 16, but I wasn't ready. Then when I was 18, I was ready. I told my Dad I was going to do it the next day.

XP: How did you get to where you are now?

Melanie: I directed all my actions to my goals… I went to college in Australia, 'cause it had weather for skydiving. I moved from New York to LA to be in a skydiving community and I spent all my money on skydiving. I didn't see any obstacles on my way. At age 27, I was able to quit my job and start full-time at Skydive Elsinore.

XP: Do you want to try wingsuit or BASE jumping?

Melanie: Oh, no! The videos totally turn my stomach. I don't get any fun out of increased risk. I like to calculate my risk, to be as safe as possible. I love my life, so I make some choices to protect it.

XP: Any advice to the newcomers?

Melanie: Jump a lot, get good coaching and good habits make us better, and when we're better, we have more fun.

skydiving

wingsurfing

skysurfing

Based on: <http://skydivechick.com>. Accessed on: May 21, 2012.

3 Check the correct alternative.

1 What kind of text is this?

a ☐ An interview. b ☐ A biography.

2 What is the main topic?

a ☐ Traditional sports. b ☐ Non-traditional sports.

4 Write T (true) or F (false).

1 ☐ Traditional sports are not as dangerous as extreme sports.
2 ☐ Melanie Curtis is a reporter.
3 ☐ Surfing is an extreme air sport.
4 ☐ Melanie probably has good habits.
5 ☐ Melanie went to Australia to surf.
6 ☐ Wingsurfing is probably more dangerous than skydiving.

5 Answer the questions.

1 Why didn't she skydive at 16?

____

2 Why doesn't she try BASE?

____

6 Check the sport which is not considered an extreme sport.

windsurfing ☐

rock climbing ☐

beach volley ☐

Let's Talk about It

Esporte radical é aquele cujo risco é muito alto devido a vários fatores, como velocidade e altura. Por que você acha que as pessoas procuram esse tipo de esporte? Você gostaria de praticar esportes radicais? Quais? Se não, por quê?

29 **7** Listen to an interview with the Brazilian skydiver Carol Chacon. Write T (true) or F (false). Correct the false sentences.

1 [ ] Carol Chacon is 17 years old.

____

2 [ ] Nobody influenced her to practice skydiving.

____

3 [ ] Her sister is interested in skydiving.

____

4 [ ] She has never had an accident.

____

5 [ ] Carol's sister is older than her.

____

Audio based on: <www.globotv.globo.com>. Accessed on: May 22, 2012.

8 Listen to the interview again and order the sequence of events.

- [ ] Carol started practicing skydiving.
- [ ] She went to Arizona.
- [ ] Her father wanted to be a parachutist.
- [ ] Carol's mother decided to jump.
- [ ] She had a problem during a jump.

GRAMMAR

Verb Tense Review

Present Continuous: ação em andamento no presente.
We **are leaving** now.

Past Continuous: ação passada, em andamento.
She **was writing** the letter at 3 o'clock.

Simple Present: ação habitual, fato.
That kid **watches** TV every morning.

Simple Past: ação passada, terminada.
She **wrote** a letter yesterday.

Future with Going to: ação planejada ou decisão tomada.
He **is going to travel** next week.

9 Complete the sentences. Use the correct verb tense.

1 I *get* (get) back home very early every day.
2 ________ Mrs. Miller ________ (teach) Math in your school?
3 We ________ (walk) to school yesterday morning.
4 What ________ she ________ (cook) for lunch now?
5 We ________ (visit) the museum next holiday.
6 I ________ (study) when the bell rang.

10 Write questions. The underlined parts are the answers.

1 The kids were eating <u>lollipops</u>.

____

2 The women are having lunch <u>in the dining room</u>.

____

3 Janet bought <u>a beautiful dress</u> yesterday.

____

4 Roger goes to the recreational club <u>at 3 o'clock</u>.

____

5 We are going to the beach <u>next week</u>.

____

6 The boys were playing <u>in the garden</u>.

____

11 Look at the pictures. Talk to a classmate.

1

money / wallet

A: *Is there any money in the wallet?*

B: *Yes, there is some.*

2

oranges / basket

A: *Are there any oranges in the basket?*

B: *No, there aren't any.*

3

juice / jar

4

eggs / box

5

salt / pot

6

tomatoes / table

7

milk / glass

8

salad / refrigerator

12 Write sentences about the pictures in exercise 11.

1 money *There is some money in the wallet.*

2 oranges *There aren't any oranges in the basket.*

3 juice ______________________________

4 eggs ______________________________

5 salt ______________________________

6 tomatoes ______________________________

7 milk ______________________________

8 salad ______________________________

GRAMMAR

Some / Any

Some (algum/ns, alguma/s) é usado em frases afirmativas.
Take **some** sugar in the sugar pot.
There are **some** eggs in the basket.

Some também é usado em frases interrogativas, quando se espera uma resposta positiva.
Would you like **some** tea?
Can I have **some** ice cream, Mom?

Any (algum/ns, alguma/s) é usado em frases interrogativas e negativas.
Do you have **any** idea?
I didn't see **any** eggs on the table.

13 Complete the sentences. Use *some* or *any*.

1 Would you like ______________ coffee?
2 Do they have ______________ pets?
3 She didn't buy ______________ fruit at the market.
4 There were ______________ teachers in the lab.
5 Do you eat ______________ vegetables?
6 I can't go out today. I have ______________ homework to do.
7 There isn't ______________ students in the classroom.

14 Rewrite the sentences. Use the cues given.

1 There isn't any sugar in the pot.
(affirmative) ______________________________
2 Do you have any information about the accident?
(negative) ______________________________
3 She doesn't have any money with her.
(affirmative) ______________________________
4 We can see some students playing in the gym.
(interrogative) ______________________________
5 Does he have any free time?
(negative) ______________________________
6 She bought some books yesterday.
(interrogative) ______________________________

15 Read the sentences below. Write C (correct) or W (wrong). Rewrite the wrong ones.

1 [W] The children ate any candies yesterday.
The children ate some candies yesterday.

2 [ ] I didn't see any cats on the roof.

____

3 [ ] Did he write some messages to you?

____

4 [ ] Would you like any coffee?

____

5 [ ] They can bring some juice to the picnic.

____

6 [ ] Do you see some children in the park?

____

16 Ian, Syl and Carol are chatting. Write your name and take part into the conversation.

Address: www.chatinbox.com Search

Ian:	What are you going to do this weekend?
Carol:	I'm going to the beach.
Ian:	Do you surf?
Carol:	No, I don't.
You:	I'm going to the mountains.
Syl:	What are you going to do there, ______________ (your name)?
You:	
Carol:	What did you do last weekend, ______________ (your name)?
You:	
Ian:	What did you do last weekend, Syl?
Syl:	I studied Math with Erica.
You:	What are you going to do next weekend, Ian?
Ian:	I'm going to the mall. What about you?
You:	
Carol:	Bye, folks. I have to go.
Ian:	Bye, see you.
You:	

FUN

17 Write the names of some extreme sports.

X Sports

6 letters:

7 letters:

8 letters:

9 letters:

11 letters:

12 letters:

Key Language

any	expose	have	some	start	try
dangerous	go	like	sports	tells	want

Way to Go

1 Read an extract of the book *Grandpa*. Write the verbs in parentheses in the Simple Present, Present Continuous or Past Continuous.

"How'________ (be) your mom?" Denise asked.

"She ________________ (get) better." Clara answered. "The doctor ________________ (tell) her she will be OK if she ________________ (continue) the treatment."

The two girls ________________ (talk) in Clara's bedroom. They ________________ (be) both seventeen and they were cousins. Their parents were in the living room.

"What ________________ you ________________ (think) our folks ________________ (talk) about?" asked Denise.

"I don't know, but it must be serious," replied Clara.

"Yeah, my mom and dad ________________ (seem) worried," Denise said.

"Mine too... But, anyhow... you said you ________________ (have) something to tell me. So, what is it?" Clara ________________ (be) curious. [...]

Extracted from: AMOS, Eduardo; PRESCHER, Elisabeth; PASQUALIN, Ernesto. *Grandpa*. São Paulo: Richmond Publishing, 2003. p. 3.

2 Read the extract in exercise 1 again. Answer the questions below.

1 What is the relationship between Denise and Clara?

____

2 Why can the reader infer that Clara's mother is sick?

____

3 Why are the girls worried?

____

3 Complete the dialogues. Use *some* or *any*.

1 **A:** Hey, Thomas. I'm hungry and thirsty. I'm going to eat ________________ pasta and drink ________________ cold juice. Want ________________?

B: Yeah! Do you have ________________ pizza?

A: Sorry, but I don't have ________________. What about a hamburger?

B: Great!

2 **A:** Are there ________________ bakeries around here?

B: Sure. What do you want to buy?

A: I want ________________ bread and ________________ peanut butter. ________________ suggestion of a good bakery for that?

B: Yeah, go to Magic Bread.

4 Read the magazine cover below. Copy the headlines that refer to:

1 fashion ______________________________

2 make-up ______________________________

3 facts of private life ______________________________

5 What do the numbers below refer to? Check the correct alternative.

1 400

a ☐ Years. b ☐ Money. c ☐ Pages.

2 100

a ☐ Ways to combine clothes and accessories. c ☐ Stores to buy nice dresses.

b ☐ Ways to spend money.

6 Who are the people most probably interested in this magazine? Answer in Portuguese.

____

____

Extra Reading 1

Address: www.buzzle.com

Search

healthandhealth

Sport and Physical Activity for a Healthy Lifestyle

Sports are excellent physical activities that provide the body with a variety of health benefits. Sports help reduce blood sugar level and the risk of blood cholesterol, strengthen the bones and muscles and tone the body. That's why people who play sports have a very positive body image. They also have fewer chances of hypertension and other stress disorders. In fact, these people can deal with stresses in life in a better manner. Depression, anxiety and other psychological disorders are less prevalent in people who are involved in sport activities. The benefits are not only physical: playing sports improves Math skills in children and teenagers, develops leadership qualities and creates a cooperative atmosphere.

Since sports involve competition, they expose players to both aspects of life: accomplishments and failures. They teach people to accept successes and disappointments, interact with other people, act as a team, think collectively and develop confidence and planning skills. Playing sports is a mixture of recreation and physical activity that can substantially improve the quality of life.

Based on: <www.buzzle.com>. Accessed on: February 15, 2012.

1. Check the statement that is not true according to the text.

1 ☐ People learn how to deal with disappointments when they practice sports.

2 ☐ Sports are good for people interaction.

3 ☐ People who play sports tend to be stressed because of competition.

4 ☐ Sports benefits are physical and mental.

2. Now, answer the question below.

How can sports help the body?

____

____

PROJECT

Olympic Sports

In groups, choose one of the Olympic sports below.

Do some research on it. Some references for research are:

- <www.london2012.com>
- <www.olympic.org>
- <http://espn.go.com>

Make a page for a catalogue about the sport you choose. Give information about it and pictures to illustrate the folder.

Don't forget to cite the sources of the text and images that you use in your project. If you use your own photos or drawings, don't forget to mention that either.

Follow your teacher's instructions.

Extra Reading 2

Digital Inclusion in Brazil: What's the Real Thing?

1 Brazilian government and society are aware of the digital divide presently experienced by millions of Brazilians. The advances in digital inclusion in Brazil are still emerging and precarious, but both the Brazilian state and society have started a sequence of positive initiatives to diminish the digital divide.

2 A study from 2003, based on data from the Brazilian Institute of Geography and Statistics (IBGE), showed that, at the time, only 12.46 per cent of the Brazilian population had access to computers and the number of internet users was lower, at 8.31 per cent. This number was a little higher in 2007 (27 per cent) and it improved in 2011 (48 per cent), according to Fecomércio-RJ/Ipsos.

3 According to the FGV data, there is a "digital apartheid" in Brazil, which means that the typical computer user is white, lives in large cities in the South and the Southeast of the country, has a salary above the national average, and has studied for about 12 years. The survey shows that computer and internet use was superior amongst Class A, the top of the Brazilian wealth pyramid, with 89 per cent of all users. The amount is lower amongst Class B (56 per cent) and it decreases amongst lower-income people from Classes C (16 per cent) and D (2 per cent).

4 In 2000, community telecenters started in the city of São Paulo, in the Capão Redondo district. The Telecentro Chico Mendes was established in 2001 in Porto Alegre, the capital of the southern state of Rio Grande do Sul. Porto Alegre and São Paulo are pioneers in setting up digital inclusion structures at a local level. Such initiatives are based on involvement and participation of the Third Sector entities.

5 Besides that, Workshops for Digital Inclusion are the center for discussion and exchange of experiences among government, activists and telecenter organizers. The discussions from numerous workshops that took place over the years allowed the creation of the key policies sustaining the Telecentros.br Program, created in 2010, to fight the digital divide in Brazil.

Based on: <http://itdecs.com>; <http://tobeguarany.com>. Accessed on: February 15, 2012.

1 In which paragraph can you find the information below?

1 The first real telecenter initiatives in two Brazilian cities:

____

2 The data of the IBGE study:

____

3 The program created after Workshops for Digital Inclusion:

____

4 Digital divide data in economical classes:

____

2 Read the text again and write down what the underlined words refer to:

1 This number <u>was a little higher in 2007</u>.

____

2 Such initiatives <u>are based on involvement and participation of the Third Sector entities</u>.

____

3 Write T (true) or F (false) according to the text.

1 [ ] Brazilian government doesn't know anything about Brazilians' digital division.

2 [ ] Most of Brazilians had access to computers by 2003.

3 [ ] According to FGV, it's more common to have people from the South and the Southeast of Brazil using computers.

4 [ ] The establishment of some telecenters in São Paulo and Rio Grande do Sul are based on actions of the Third Sector entities.

PROJECT

Telecenters in My Community

Do some research on the Telecenters in your community. Some references for research are:

- <www.onid.org.br/mapa>
- <www.onid.org.br/portal/programas>

Organize the information you get on a poster and bring it to your class.

Don't forget to mention the sources of the text and images that you use in your project. If you use your own photos or drawings, don't forget to mention that either.

Follow your teacher's instructions.

Extra Reading 3

Planet News 18

Around Us

Indigenous People in Brazil

There are about 200 indigenous societies living in Brazil: 200 different cultures with diverse languages, religions and social groups. This is one of the greatest cultural treasures of the world, but this treasure, unfortunately, is under continual risk, mainly because of the conflicts over land and the subsequent invasions.

The lower-quality artifacts the Indians produce are a good example of non-Indian influence on Indian people. The raw materials that are necessary for the production of their art are not available because of environmental changes. Besides that, low investment in education and healthcare leave some indigenous societies vulnerable to regional influences and at the mercy of benefits from the government.

The Pataxó Hã-Hã-Hãe, who live in the south of the state of Bahia, had their physical space destroyed and their local flora reduced. That affected the production of their artifacts that were ornate in feathers of the birds from the region. The feathers used today are of common birds, dyed with bright colors, which don't represent the true Pataxó culture. Nowadays, they produce works to collect resources that will allow them to consume products and goods produced by non-Indians. Experts in the art of weaving, the Fulnio Indians, from Pernambuco, face a similar situation. They have problems in finding raw materials to produce baskets, mats and other pieces. They also work with wood, making bowls, combs and other objects for later sale. The pressure from civilization, however, has not changed their religious beliefs or influenced the social organization of the group. They are concerned about maintaining their language, continuing with their rituals and teaching the youngsters their traditions.

The Funai's (Fundação Nacional do Índio) Indian Memory project, in 1994, which consisted of registering cultural values, developed activities with the native cultures to guarantee technical and scientific support for the production of objects and artifacts that symbolize each group's specialty. The Indian Memory project also intended to organize collections of different cultures of the Brazilian tribal groups. This mission for preservation and restoration of indigenous values was not new at the time: various tribes that live in the mid-west were also helped by this project.

Based on: <www.brasilsf.org>. Accessed on: July 18, 2012.

1 Scan the article, find the correct information and write it below.

1 The Brazilian foundation created to protect the indigenous people:

___

2 The project created to preserve the Indians' culture:

___

3 An indigenous tribe in the south of Bahia:

___

4 Approximate number of Indian cultures living in Brazil:

___

2 What could be an alternative title for this text?

1 [ ] Good News for Indians in Brazil

2 [ ] The Memory of a Culture

3 [ ] Indians and Arts

PROJECT

Brazilian Indigenous Tribes

In groups, choose one of the Brazilian indigenous tribes below.

- Fulnio
- Krenak
- Guarani Kaiwoá
- Pataxós
- Kayapó
- Yanomani

Do some research on it. Some references for research are:

- <www.funai.gov.br>
- <www.native-languages.org>
- <www.dismalworld.com>
- <www.suapesquisa.com>

Create a photo/picture album about the indigenous tribe you choose.

Write a small paragraph under each photo/picture.

Don't forget to cite the sources of the text and images that you use in your project. If you use your own photos or drawings, don't forget to mention that either.

Follow your teacher's instructions.

Extra Reading 4

Address: www.birdtricks.com

Search

BLUE MACAW

STATUS
Endangered species.

FEATURES
Large, blue, plumage, with large black bill and a movable upper mandible, a yellow eye-ring.

PREDATORS
Few predators, apart from humans, sometimes captured by harpy eagles.

DIET
Fruit, seeds, nuts and roots.

HABITAT
Wooded rainforest of South America.

REPRODUCTION
Sexual maturity: four to six years of age.
Breeding periods: October to February.
Nests: in tree trunks or on cliff sides.

BEHAVIOR
They eat limestone from cliffs to neutralize toxins in some seeds. Only a few thousand hyacinth macaws are living in small groups in South America.

AT THE BIODOME
They do not often reproduce in captivity. They interact a great deal with each other. They sometimes regurgitate food into another macaw's mouth. Their call is very loud.

Based on: <www2.ville.montreal.qc.ca>; <www.bluemacaws.org>; <www.birdtricks.com>. Accessed on: February 17, 2012.

Unit 2

There to Be (haver, existir)

Usamos *there to be* para:

- indicar que alguma coisa existe:

  There are three bedrooms in my apartment.

- indicar quantidade:

  There are 22 rooms in that hotel.

There is/are (existe(m), há)

Affirmative

Singular: **There is** a drugstore next to my house.
Plural: **There are** ten boys in my classroom.

Negative

Singular: **There is not** a calculator in my schoolbag.
Plural: **There are not** any sausages in the fridge.

Interrogative

Singular: **Is there** a good movie on TV today?
Plural: **Are there** biscuits and soft drinks for the children?

Short answers

Yes, **there is**. / No, **there isn't**.
Yes, **there are**. / No, **there aren't**.

Formas abreviadas

There's = There is
There isn't = There is not
There aren't = There are not

There was/were (existia(m), havia)

Affirmative

Singular: **There was** a charitable bingo at the club last night.
Plural: **There were** a lot of children at the party.

Negative

Singular: **There wasn't** a school on this street in 2003.
Plural: **There weren't** good dancers in our last school talent show.

Interrogative

Singular: **Was there** a teacher at school last Saturday?
Plural: **Were there** restaurants at the shopping mall?

Short answers

Yes, **there was**. / No, **there wasn't**.
Yes, **there were**. / No, **there weren't**.

Formas abreviadas

There wasn't = There was not
There weren't = There were not

1 Use the expressions in the box to complete the sentences.

are there
There aren't
There is
There isn't
There was
there were
Were th

1 ______________ a ruler under your notebook. Can you lend it to me?

2 ______________ lots of people in front of the museum yesterday morning?

3 ______________ eggs in the fridge. I need to go out to buy a dozen for the cake.

4 How many windows ______________ in your living room?

5 ______________ ovie theater near our house, let's go downtown.

ast summer ______________ a lot of monkeys at the city zoo.

______________ a big party on my last birthday.

Personal Pronouns – Review

Os *Personal Pronouns* correspondem aos *Subject Pronouns* e *Object Pronouns* em inglês.

Os *Subject Pronouns* são usados como sujeito das orações. Em português, eles correspondem aos pronomes pessoais do caso reto.

Os *Object Pronouns* são usados como objeto direto ou indireto; eles vêm após verbos ou preposições. Em português, eles correspondem aos pronomes pessoais do caso oblíquo.

Subject Pronouns		Object Pronouns	
I	(1ª pessoa do singular)	**me**	(1ª pessoa do singular)
you	(2ª pessoa do singular)	**you**	(2ª pessoa do singular)
he / **she** / **it**	(3ª pessoa do singular)	**him** / **her** / **it**	(3ª pessoa do singular)
we	(1ª pessoa do plural)	**us**	(1ª pessoa do plural)
you	(2ª pessoa do plural)	**you**	(2ª pessoa do plural)
they	(3ª pessoa do plural)	**them**	(3ª pessoa do plural)

Elisa and I were at the park with **Carlos**.
We were at the park with **him**.

Robert loves **Julia**.
He loves **her**.

2 Underline the appropriate Subject or Object Pronouns.

1 Mom is coming. Look at **she** / **her**!

2 Those are my favorite books. Give **they** / **them** back to **I** / **me** as soon as possible.

3 I think **he** / **him** is behind the curtains! Let's find **he** / **him**!

4 **We** / **Us** are very upset with Ted. He never calls **we** / **us** to share the good news.

5 **I** / **Me** am very glad you can join **I** / **me** for lunch today!

Unit 3

Simple Past

Usamos o *Simple Past* para indicar ações concluídas em um tempo definido no passado.

Em sentenças afirmativas, o *Simple Past* dos verbos regulares é formado acrescentando-se *ed*, *d* ou *ied* ao infinitivo dos verbos.

I **visited** my grandma last weekend.
She **lived** downtown when she was twenty.
They **called** me yesterday morning.

Em sentenças negativas, o auxiliar *did* + *not* é posicionado após o sujeito, em todas as pessoas, seguido pelo verbo no infinitivo sem *to*.

I **did not visit** my grandma last weekend.

A forma abreviada de *did not* é *didn't*.

She **didn't live** downtown when she was twenty.

Em sentenças interrogativas, o auxiliar *did* é seguido pelo sujeito e o verbo no infinitivo sem *to*.

Did I **visit** my grandma last weekend?
Did she **live** downtown when she was twenty?

Short answers

Yes, you **did**. / No, you **didn't**.
Yes, she **did**. / No, she **didn't**.
Yes, they **did**. / No, they **didn't**.

Spelling rules

À maioria dos verbos regulares, acrescenta-se *ed* ao infinitivo:

enter = enter**ed** talk = talk**ed**

Aos verbos terminados em *e*, acrescenta-se somente *d*:

dance = dance**d** love = love**d**

Aos verbos terminados em *y* precedido por uma consoante, troca-se o *y* por *ied*:

study = stud**ied** cry = cr**ied**

Aos verbos de uma só sílaba ou terminados em sílaba tônica formada por *consoante* + *vogal* + *consoante*, dobra-se a última consoante e acrescenta-se *ed*.

stop = stop**ped** drop = drop**ped**

1 Use the cues to ask and answer questions in the Simple Past. Give complete answers.

1 Carlos / wait for us / for a long time / yesterday / last week

Did Carlos wait for us for a long time yesterday?

No, he didn't wait for us for a long time yesterday. He waited for us for a long time last week.

2 those women / cook dinner / on Saturday / on Friday

____

____

3 you / work late / two days ago / two weeks ago

____

____

4 Henry / travel to Cancun / in 2011 / in 2012

____

____

5 we / study Physics / on Tuesday / yesterday

____

____

Unit 4

Simple Past – Irregular Verbs

Os verbos irregulares não seguem a regra geral acrescentando-se *ed*, *d* ou *ied* ao infinitivo do verbo para formação do *Simple Past* em sentenças afirmativas. Eles têm uma forma própria:

swim = **swam** I **swam** 5 laps last class.

do = **did** He **did** all his homework in the morning.

go = **went** We **went** to school by bus yesterday.

have = **had** They **had** a beautiful wedding ceremony.

Usamos o auxiliar *did* na forma interrogativa e *did not* (*didn't*) na forma negativa.

What did Mrs. Andrade teach last class?	She taught English.
Where did they take the kids?	They took the kids to the park.
When did you fly to New York?	I flew to New York last summer.
Who did he meet?	He met his girlfriend Thamires.
How much sugar **did** you bring?	I brought 3 kilos.
How much did the CD cost?	It cost 15 dollars.
How many hours **did** we sleep?	We slept 8 hours.

1 Unscramble the words to write questions. Then use the cues in the box to answer them.

50 e-mails | at 7 o'clock | by train | home appliances | my friend Carlos | the Emergency Room

1 last night / Where / go / did / doctors / the / ?

____

____

2 at the movies / did / Who / see / you / yesterday / ?

____

____

3 Andrea / did / home / How / come / ?

____

____

4 at the garage sale / did / What / sell / we / ?

____

____

5 Pete / wake up / did / What time / ?

____

____

6 e-mails / did / send / How many / they / ?

____

____

Unit 5

Past Continuous

O *Past Continuous* é usado para indicar ações que estavam em andamento em um determinado momento no passado ou para narrar circunstâncias de uma situação no passado.

At 6 o'clock in the morning, we **were driving** to our beach house.

Yesterday I got up early; it **was raining** and I decided to stay in bed.

Affirmative

I **was drinking** coffee yesterday at 8:00.

They **were working** hard last night.

Negative

I **was not taking a bath** yesterday at 8:00.

They **were not working** hard last night.

Interrogative

Was he **running** fast in the competition yesterday?

Were they **studying** Math last night?

Short answers

Yes, he **was**. / No, he **wasn't**.

Yes, they **were**. / No, they **weren't**.

Formas abreviadas

wasn't = was not

weren't = were not

1 Use the Past Continuous of the verbs in parentheses to complete the dialogues.

1 A: ______________ you ______________ (listen) to music at 10 p.m. last night?

B: No, I wasn't. I ______________ (sleep) in my bedroom.

2 A: I ______________ (swim) in my pool at this time yesterday.

B: Lucky you! My friends and I ______________ (have) a Geography test at school.

3 A: Kate ______________ (wait – neg.) for Gary at the gate.

B: Yeah. She ______________ (finish) her homework.

4 A: Why ______________ Robert ______________ (watch) that volleyball game at school?

B: Because his friends ______________ (play) and he ______________ (root) for them.

5 A: ______________ you two ______________ (argue) a minute ago?

B: Of course we ______________ (argue – neg.). We ______________ just ______________ (talk).

6 A: Hi, Janet. What ______________ (do) yesterday night while your brothers ______________ (watch) the basketball game between our school team and the Star Boys? I didn't see you at the gym.

B: Actually, I forgot about the game. I ______________ (study) for the Spanish test.

A: Good for you. The game was awful for our team!

Past Continuous

Usamos o *Past Continuous* para expressar ações que estavam em andamento simultaneamente em um momento do passado ou quando uma ação estava em andamento quando outra ação ocorreu. Nesses casos, é comum o uso dos advérbios *while* e *when*.

while: enquanto

The teacher **was correcting** compositions **while** the students **were doing** grammar exercises.

when: quando

The teacher **was correcting** compositions **when** the students **left** the classroom.

2 Underline the correct alternatives to complete the sentences.

1 While Dan and Thelma **were talking / talked** in the living room, the phone rang.

2 We were reading a magazine when we **were hearing / heard** a noise outside.

3 When he got to the campsite it **wasn't raining / didn't rain**.

4 Sheila **was walking / walked** around the block while her husband **was exercising / exercised** at the gym.

5 My grandparents **were playing / played** cards when my mother **was calling / called**.

6 I didn't see any lions while I **was visiting / visited** the city zoo.

7 **Were you using / Did you use** the computer while your father **was working / worked**?

Unit 6

Degrees of Comparison

Os adjetivos podem ser usados nos graus normal, comparativo e superlativo.

Comparatives

Usamos os *Comparatives* para estabelecer comparações entre seres, objetos, animais, etc. Existem 3 tipos de *Comparatives*: igualdade, inferioridade e superioridade.

- Para expressar igualdade, usamos *as + adjective + as* (tão... quanto).

  Geography is **as** interesting **as** History.

- Para expressar inferioridade, usamos *less + adjective + than* (menos... que).

  Carol is **less** beautiful **than** Ana.

- Para expressar superioridade com adjetivos de duas ou mais sílabas, usamos *more + adjective + than* (mais... que).

  A lion is **more** dangerous **than** a cat.

Superlatives

Usamos os *Superlatives* para expressar o mais alto ou baixo grau de um adjetivo, para intensificar certa característica.

- Para adjetivos com mais de uma sílaba, usamos *the least + adjective* (o menos...).

  Spanish is **the least** difficult subject at school.

- Para adjetivos com mais de uma sílaba, usamos *the most + adjective* (o mais...).

  The bank managers booked **the most** expensive hotel rooms.

1 Choose the best alternative to complete the sentences.

1 Anette's clothes ________________ my clothes.

a ☐ are more fashionable than b ☐ the most fashionable

2 Math is ________________ subject in my opinion.

a ☐ more difficult than b ☐ the most difficult

3 I stayed at ________________ hotel in São Paulo.

a ☐ less expensive than b ☐ the least expensive

4 Was yesterday ________________ today?

a ☐ as hot as b ☐ the least hot

Tag Questions

As *Tag Questions* são perguntas curtas usadas ao final das sentenças para confirmar o que foi dito anteriormente. São formadas por um verbo auxiliar e um pronome.

Para definir o auxiliar que comporá a *Tag Question*, é preciso identificar o tempo verbal da oração principal. Se a oração principal for negativa, a *Tag Question* será afirmativa; se a oração principal for afirmativa, a *Tag Question* será negativa.

You are my best friend, **aren't you**?

They didn't come to class yesterday, **did they**?

Terry is going to buy a new apartment, **isn't he**?

Chris always travels on her vacations, **doesn't she**?

We closed the door, **didn't we**?

You weren't here in April, **were you**?

She can't speak German, **can she**?

Casos especiais

I am helpful, **aren't I**?

Let's stop and rest, **shall we**?

Shut up, **will you**?

2 Read the sentences below. Write the appropriate Tag Questions.

1 You are going to come to my party, ______________________________?
2 I can't turn on the air conditioning, ______________________________?
3 She likes Paul, ______________________________?
4 They won't help us, ______________________________?
5 We were playing tennis, ______________________________?
6 John doesn't have to get up early, ______________________________?
7 The boys left early, ______________________________?

Unit 7

Degrees of Comparison

Para expressar o comparativo de superioridade com adjetivos de uma sílaba, acrescentamos a terminação *er* ao adjetivo.

er + than: mais... do que

July is **colder than** January in the south of Brazil.
A bike is **slower than** a car.

Para expressar o superlativo de adjetivos de uma sílaba, acrescentamos a eles a terminação *est* e o adjetivo é precedido de *the*.

the... est: o mais...

February is **the shortest** month of the year.
I want to buy **the smallest** dress in the store.

Spelling rules

Na forma comparativa, em adjetivos terminados em *y*, troca-se o *y* por *i* e acrescenta-se *er*. No superlativo, em adjetivos terminados em *y*, troca-se o *y* por *i* e acrescenta-se *est*.

angry = angr**ier** / the angr**iest**
hungry = hungr**ier** / the hungr**iest**

Em adjetivos terminados em *consoante* + *vogal* + *consoante*, dobra-se a consoante final e acrescenta-se *er* para o comparativo e *est* para o superlativo.

hot = hot**ter** / the hot**test**
sad = sad**der** / the sad**dest**

Irregular Comparatives and Superlatives

Adjectives	Comparatives	Superlatives
good	better	the best
bad	worse	the worst
far	farther / further	the farthest / the furthest

1 Use the Adjectives in parentheses in the comparative or superlative forms to complete the sentences.

1 For me, Friday is ____________________ (good) Sunday.
2 Andrew is ____________________ (hungry) boy in our group. He's always eating something.
3 Uncle Carl is ____________________ (old) aunt Joanna, but he isn't ____________________ (old) man in our family.
4 Did you read ____________________ (late) issue of *People* magazine?
5 We are ____________________ (sad) our classmates because we didn't pass the midterm exams.

Unit 8

Verb Tense – Review

O *Present Continuous* é usado para expressar uma ação que está (ou não) acontecendo no momento da fala:

We **are studying** English now.
Are we **studying** English now?
We **aren't studying** English now.

O *Past Continuous* é usado para expressar uma ação que estava (ou não) acontecendo em um tempo determinado no passado:

I **was reading** a book last night.
Was Izabella **talking** to her friend Renata last night?
The kids **weren't playing** soccer this morning.

O *Simple Present* é usado para expressar uma ação rotineira ou um fato:

The girl **walks** to school every weekday.
Does it **rain** every summer?
The teachers **don't go** to school on Sundays.

O *Simple Past* é usado para expressar uma ação concluída e com tempo definido no passado:

They **sang** at the school party last semester.
Did the Lawsons **go** to the beach a month ago?
The students **didn't bring** the books to school yesterday.

O *Future with going to* é usado para expressar planos ou intenções para o futuro, ações que acontecerão em um futuro próximo.

He **is going to apply** for a private university next year.
Is Arthur **going to move** to a bigger apartment in September?
My family **isn't going to visit** Rome next vacations.

1 Use the verbs in parentheses in the appropriate tenses to complete the sentences below.

1 That woman always ________________ (water) her garden in the morning.
2 ________________ you ________________ (go) to the movies last weekend?
3 I'm ________________ (not buy) new uniforms for the kids next year.
4 We were ________________ (come) back to the office when the boss called us.

Some / Any

Os *Indefinite Pronouns some* e *any* são usados para indicar quantidades indefinidas.

Some (algum, alguns, alguma, algumas) é usado quando se oferece algo a alguém, em frases afirmativas ou interrogativas, acompanhando substantivos contáveis ou incontáveis, no singular ou no plural.

There are **some** oranges in the bowl.
Would you like **some** salt?

Any (algum, alguns, alguma, algumas, nenhum, nenhuma) é usado em frases negativas ou interrogativas, acompanhando substantivos contáveis ou incontáveis, no singular ou no plural.

There aren't **any** books on the shelves.
Are there **any** doctors at the clinic today?

Any (qualquer) também pode ser usado em frases afirmativas.

The teacher said we can ask **any** questions during her explanation.

2 Circle the correct alternative to complete the sentences.

1 I need to buy **some** / **any** bananas to make the pie.
2 He didn't bring **some** / **any** books to class yesterday.
3 Did we make **some** / **any** mistakes?
4 Can you lend me **some** / **any** money?
5 Andrea didn't make **some** / **any** new friends on her trip abroad.

Workbook

Name:

Number: Class: Date:

1 Fill in the blanks with the correct form of the verb *to be* in the Simple Past.

1 I ______________ very tired yesterday.

2 My brother and I ______________ at home in the afternoon.

3 The children ______________ at school because yesterday was Sunday. (neg.)

4 Susan ______________ at the shopping mall last Saturday afternoon. (neg.)

2 Rewrite the sentences in the Simple Past.

1 I am at school.

____

2 Mrs. Johnson is very tired.

____

3 The weather isn't good.

____

4 My parents are not at home.

____

3 Ask questions and answer them.

1 Anna / at the supermarket / yesterday afternoon (Yes)
Was Anna at the supermarket yesterday afternoon?
Yes, she was.

2 My grandma / happy / last Sunday (No)

____

____

3 My mother and my father / born / in 1970 (Yes)

____

____

4 you / at the park / very early this morning (No)

____

____

4 Answer the questions below.

1 When were you born?

____

2 Where were you yesterday morning?

____

3 When was the last time you were at the beach?

____

4 How were you last Sunday afternoon?

____

5 How old was your mother when you were born?

____

6 Where were you and your brother / sister last weekend?

____

5 Read an extract of Madonna's biography. Answer the questions.

Madonna was born in Bay City, Michigan, U.S., on August 16, 1958. In 1981 she became a sensation as a pop singer. In 1983, she produced the album *Madonna*. Some of the hit singles were "Borderline", "Lucky Star", and "Holiday".
Her next album was *Like a Virgin*, in 1985, which hit number 1 on the Billboard chart. In 2012, the singer sold 359,000 records of the album called *MDNA*.

Based on: <www.biography.com>. Accessed on: June 6, 2012.

1 When was Madonna born?

____

2 Which were some of Madonna's hit singles in 1983?

____

3 What was the name of Madonna's number 1 album on the Billboard chart in 1985?

____

4 What's the name of Madonna's album released in 2012?

____

Workbook

Name:

Number: | Class: | Date:

1 Read the dialogues below. Check the places where the people have to go.

1 **A:** Chris, today is Dad's birthday. We need to buy him a present.

B: Yeah. What about a beautiful shirt?

a ☐ shopping mall
b ☐ bakery
c ☐ restaurant

2 **A:** I'm hungry. Let's have a snack.

B: Yeah, OK.

a ☐ church
b ☐ bakery
c ☐ square

3 **A:** Bob, I need to get some money. Can you give me a ride?

B: Yes, of course.

a ☐ theater
b ☐ playground
c ☐ bank

2 Complete the sentences. Use the verb *there to be* in the Simple Past.

1 ______________________ many people at the restaurant at about 1 o'clock.

2 ______________________ a hole in the middle of the street.

3 ______________________ a library at school?

4 ______________________ many pictures on the wall?

5 ______________________ many people at the gym on Saturday. Almost everybody was at the pool.

6 ______________________ a chair in the room. The room was empty.

7 ______________________ any books on the shelves?

3 Unscramble the words to form sentences.

1 yesterday / three / There / were / apples / table / on / the / .

____

2 supermarket / school / near / the / Was / there / a / ?

____

3 cell phone / backpack / a / There / was / my / in / .

____

4 an / ago / There / children / park / at / the / five / were / half / hour / .

____

5 there / boxes / cookies / shelf / Were / ten / of / the / on / ?

____

6 was / There / a / brown / of / basket / big / fruit / table / on / the / .

____

4 Fill in the blanks with the appropriate Pronoun.

1 I need to buy a pair of jeans. How much are ______________?

2 This is an easy exercise. I don't have to worry about ______________.

3 I have to buy some fruit and vegetables. ______________ am going to buy ______________ at the supermarket.

4 Susan doesn't know what to buy for dinner. ______________ has to ask her mother.

5 My Geography teacher's name is Mr. Johnson. ______________ like ______________ very much.

6 Malena's children love books. Her son Jason reads one book each week. ______________ says books provide hours of surprise and discovery. His sister Deena agrees with ______________. ______________ also reads a book each week.

5 Underline the best options to complete the sentences below.

1 **There was** / **There were** a terrible earthquake in Japan in 2005.

2 The cake **were** / **was** in the refrigerator when I arrived home.

3 How many people **were there** / **was there** at the party?

4 Our English teacher **were** / **was** angry because we didn't do our homework.

5 **Was** / **Where** there someone waiting for you at the entrance door?

6 There **weren't** / **wasn't** two books in my backpack, there **was** / **were** just some old notebooks.

Workbook

Name:

Number: Class: Date:

1 Complete the sentences. Use the Simple Past of the verbs in the box.

eat go not drink not study
play prepare wash watch

1 I ______ volleyball last weekend.
2 What movie ______ you ______ last Thursday?
3 Suzana ______ for the test.
4 My mother ______ all my clothes this morning.
5 I ______ a nice salad for lunch.
6 Phoebe ______ two pieces of pizza, but she ______ any soda.
7 ______ you ______ to Mark's birthday party last Saturday?

2 Write questions to the underlined parts.

1 *What did the boy wash?*
The boy washed his bike this morning.

2 ______
I visited my friends last Saturday.

3 ______
The girl watched a movie last night.

4 ______
They played soccer yesterday.

5 ______
Oscar prepared lunch three days ago.

6 ______
Janet's children went to the amusement park the day before yesterday.

7 ______
I arrived late for dinner yesterday because the traffic was awful!

3 Answer the questions using the words in parentheses.

1 Who visited you last week? (grandpa)

____

2 Where did the pilot disappear? (Bermuda Triangle)

____

3 What time did the plane arrive? (at 7 p.m.)

____

4 How did she travel to Europe? (ship)

____

5 What did the teacher show the students? (new computer program)

____

4 Read the e-mail below. Write T (true) or F (false).

To: jenny.stevens@popmail.com
Subject: Last weekend

Send Attach

Last weekend I traveled to the mountains with my friends. The weather was not good. It was rainy and cold. We had planned the trip so many weeks before that we did not want to cancel it. There were five of us and we rented a house in Campos do Jordão. We traveled by car and we took our bikes in the car. We wanted to ride our bikes every day but the weather did not allow us to do that. We carried our cameras everywhere. We had so many nice photos at the end of the weekend.

1 ☐ We traveled to the beach.
2 ☐ The weather was great in Campos do Jordão.
3 ☐ There were five people in the group.
4 ☐ We took our bikes in the car.
5 ☐ We wanted to ride our bikes every day.

Workbook

Name:

Number: | Class: | Date:

1 Complete the questions below. Use the question words given.

How many How much Where Who

1 ______________ sandwiches did you eat?
2 ______________ did you buy this jacket? Was it at Magic Sports store?
3 ______________ did you pay for this bicycle?
4 ______________ did you write that e-mail to?

2 Use the parts in the boxes to write meaningful sentences.

I didn't write the e-mail	my car	those sunglasses?
Where did	you buy	for dinner.
Yesterday I ate	the newspaper	this morning?
My friend Joe drove	because the internet	was not connecting.
Did you read	pizza	last weekend.

1 ______________

2 ______________

3 ______________

4 ______________

5 ______________

3 Complete Arthur's e-mail to his friend Bob. Use the verbs in parentheses in the Simple Past.

To: bob@xmail.com
Subject: Last Saturday

Send Attach

Hi, Bob,

I am writing to you to tell you about the trip I ____________ (make) last weekend. When I ____________ (get up) on Saturday morning the weather ____________ (be) not good. I ____________ (think) "I am not going anymore". But I ____________ (read) on the internet that it would not be cold. Then, I ____________ (drive) to the beach where I have a small house. I ____________ (bring) my raincoat just in case. When I ____________ (arrive) there I ____________ (ride) my bike and ____________ (play) volleyball on the beach. I ____________ (eat) fish at a very nice restaurant. In the evening, I ____________ (buy) some chocolate ice cream and ____________ (go) home. I also ____________ (drink) some soft drinks I ____________ (have) in the fridge. It ____________ (be) a nice and relaxing day. It ____________ (be) a pity you didn't go there.

I hope you can go next time.

Bye for now,

Arthur

4 Read the text again. Answer the questions.

1 What was the weather like on Saturday morning?

____

2 Where did Arthur go on the weekend?

____

3 What did he do when he arrived there?

____

4 What did he eat?

____

5 What did he do in the evening?

____

Workbook

Name:

Number: | Class: | Date:

1 Fill in the blanks with the verbs in parentheses in the Past Continuous.

1 I ________________ (watch) TV when she called.

2 What ________________ you ________________ (do) when I arrived?

3 Sammy ________________ (wait – neg.) for us when we got off the plane.

4 When I ________________ (write) the e-mail, the phone rang.

2 Make sentences in the Past.

1 I / listen to music / my mother / arrive

I was listening to music when my mother arrived.

2 it / start to rain / we / have a picnic

____

3 the computer / suddenly break down/ I / write the e-mail

____

4 you / do / earthquake start

____

3 Check the best alternative to complete the text message below.

Hi, Janet! Yesterday our classmates ________________ to throw a farewell party for Mr. Geller, the Spanish teacher. I ________________ the guest list when Jack ________________ that you are a wonderful cook and can make delicious cakes. Can you help us with that? Benny ________________ me from the mall a few minutes ago and said he ________________ a nice present for Mr. Geller. This morning we all ________________ 10 dollars each to buy it. Can you give him 10 dollars to buy the present too? Call me ASAP.

☐ was writing decided said called gave was looking for

☐ decided was writing said called was looking for gave

☐ decided called was writing said was looking for gave

4 Look at the picture and complete the sentences below.

This is the Smiths family. They are Sarah and Wilson and their children are: Fernanda, Raul and Marcos. Raul is 14 years old. Fernanda is 10 years old. Marcos is 10 years old too. They are twins. Their father is a businessman. They were together in the living room yesterday evening.

1 ____________ and ____________ were playing video game.

2 ____________ was writing an e-mail.

3 ____________ was reading a book.

4 ____________ was talking on the phone.

5 Ask questions to the underlined parts in the sentences.

1 *Who was working until late at night?*

<u>Tom</u> was working until late at night.

2 ________________________________

Gisele <u>was playing the piano</u> yesterday evening.

3 ________________________________

The Titanic was crossing <u>the Atlantic</u> when it hit an iceberg.

4 ________________________________

Carlos was watching a mystery movie <u>last night</u> when the lights went out.

Workbook

Name:

Number: | Class: | Date:

1 Complete the sentences with the comparative form. Use the Adjectives in the box.

comfortable delicious difficult
economical expensive

1 I think Chinese is ______________________ English.
2 My motorcycle is ______________________ my car.
3 Sleeping in a hotel is ______________________ sleeping in a tent.
4 In my opinion, *feijoada* is ______________________ *acarajé*.
5 Flying is usually ______________________ traveling by bus.

2 Make sentences with the cues given. Use the superlative of the Adjectives.

1 dolphins / intelligent / animals / in the ocean
Dolphins are the most intelligent animals in the ocean.

2 Ferrari / expensive / car / in the car showroom

____

3 in my opinion / Geography / interesting / subject

____

4 for me / Patagonia / beautiful / place / in the world

____

5 I think / Cancun / sunny / place / in the world

____

3 Underline the correct alternative.

1 Portuguese is **more difficult than / the most difficult** English.
2 For me Suzana is **more intelligent than / the most intelligent** student in class.
3 My bedroom is **more comfortable than / the most comfortable** my brother's.
4 What's the **more delicious / most delicious** food in your opinion?
5 Science fiction books are **more interesting / most interesting** than novels.

4 All the sentences below are false. Use the Adjectives in parentheses to correct them.

1 A table tennis racket is bigger than a tennis racket. (small)

____

2 An elephant is lighter than a lion. (heavy)

____

3 A gold watch is cheaper than a silver watch. (expensive)

____

4 In July, São Paulo is hotter than Rio de Janeiro. (cold)

____

5 Canada is smaller than Brazil. (big)

____

6 A hippo is friendlier than a cat. (aggressive)

____

5 Complete the dialogue. Use the expressions in the box.

better happier less stressed more interesting than safer smaller (2x)

Diego: I read in the internet that people who live in ______________ cities are ______________. Do you agree?

Adriana: Sure. I think there's definitely a ______________ quality of life if you live in a small city.

Diego: In ______________ cities people are ______________ and ______________. People can walk at night safely. They don't need to worry about violence.

Adriana: But for me living in a big city is ______________ living in a small one.

Diego: When I retire I plan to move to a small city.

Adriana: I think it's a good idea. I know that living in small cities means better quality of life, but I still prefer big cities…

Diego: Let's make a deal. You can spend some days with me when I move to a small city. What do you say?

Adriana: That's a good idea.

Diego: Deal!

Workbook

Name:

Number: | Class: | Date:

1 Complete the sentences. Use the comparative or superlative form of the Adjectives given.

1 Are you *older than* (old) your brother?
2 Everest is *the highest* (high) mountain on Earth.
3 Brazil is ______________________ (large) Chile.
4 My new car is ______________________ (fast) my old car.
5 What's ______________________ (good) movie you've ever seen?

2 Make sentences. Use the comparatives.

1
Brazil 8,5 million km^2
Australia 7,6 million km^2
large
Brazil is larger than Australia.

2
blue whale 150.000 kilos
white shark 2.268 kilos
heavy
____

Extracted from: <http://animals.nationalgeographic.com>. Accessed on: June 13, 2012.

3
São Paulo 15º C
Salvador 32º C
cold
____

4
São Paulo 11 million inhabitants
Rio de Janeiro 5,5 million inhabitants
populated
____

Extracted from: <www.citypopulation.de>. Accessed on: June 13, 2012.

3 Make sentences using the superlative form of the Adjectives.

1 The Cesar Palace / nice hotel / in this town

____

2 Fabio / thin person / I know

____

3 São Joaquim / cold place / in Brazil

____

4 This T-shirt / cheap / in the store

____

4 Fill in the blanks with the correct form of the Adjectives in the box.

cheaper than	less expensive	less polluted
less violent than	more impressive than	smaller than

Joana was born in San Francisco, but she moved to London a few years ago. She wrote this text comparing the two cities.

San Francisco is located in a beautiful bay. It's ______________ London. London has more theaters and museums than San Francisco. In my opinion, the architecture in London is ______________ in San Francisco. London is ______________ San Francisco. Nobody carries a gun, not even the police! Living in the States is ______________ living in England. For example, fuel is less than half the price. Food, clothes, and electronic devices are ______________ too. The public transportation in San Francisco is great. There are cable cars and electric buses, but London is ______________. As you can see, there are advantages and disadvantages of living in both cities.

5 Write T (true) or F (false) for the statements below, according to the text.

1 ☐ San Francisco is more violent than London.

2 ☐ Public transportation is very good in San Francisco.

3 ☐ There are good and bad aspects of living in both cities.

4 ☐ San Francisco is smaller than London.

Workbook

Name:

Number: Class: Date:

1 Unscramble the words to form sentences.

1 and / sisters / Do / have / you / brothers / any / ?

____

2 the / are / in / and / apples / There / some / refrigerator / oranges / some / .

____

3 you / have / you / teacher / can / help / Your / any / with / doubt / .

____

4 some / any / to / but / don't / I / want / have / chocolate, / eat / I / .

____

2 Complete the text with the correct verb tense.

Diego __________ (be) born in 1980 in New York, U.S. He __________ (move) to Boston when he __________ (be) 10 years old. His parents __________ (be) both doctors and so he __________ (decide) to go to Medical School too. Nowadays he __________ (be) a doctor. He __________ (live) in Washington, D.C. He __________ (marry) Angela two years ago. Angela __________ (work – neg.) at the moment. They're __________ (have) a baby next month. They are very happy with the fact that their family is getting bigger.

3 Read the teabag envelope below. Then answer the questions.

1 How many teabags are there in the envelope?

____

2 What is the name of the tea company?

____

3 There is one meal mentioned on the envelope. Which is it?

____

4 Where can you find more information about teas?

____

5 Can you serve the tea with some milk?

____

4 Match the words with their corresponding meaning.

1	boiling water	a	[ ]	take away
2	remove	b	[ ]	to put
3	warmed	c	[ ]	preheated
4	place	d	[ ]	a mug
5	cup	e	[1]	very hot water

Glossary

A

a um, uma

a few alguns, algumas, um, umas

a little bit um pouquinho

a lot of muito(s), muita(s)

able capaz

about cerca de, em torno de; sobre

abroad no exterior

academy academia

accept aceitar

accessed on acessado(a) em

accident acidente

according to de acordo com

action ação

activity atividade

actor ator

actress atriz

add acrescentar, adicionar

adjective adjetivo

adoption adoção

adverb advérbio

affect afetar

advice conselho

affection afeto

affectionate afetuoso(a)

affirmative afirmativo(a)

afraid com medo

after após, depois de; atrás

afternoon tarde

again de novo, novamente

age idade

ago atrás (tempo)

agree concordar

agressive agressivo(a)

aid ajuda

AIDS SIDA (Síndrome da Imunodeficiência Adquirida)

all todo(a), todos(as); tudo

allergic alérgico(a)

almost quase

also também

alternative alternativa, opção

although embora

amazing incrível

an um, uma

and e

angry bravo(a), furioso(a)

another outro(a)

answer responder; resposta

any algum(a); nenhum(a); qualquer

anymore não mais

apartment apartamento

appliance aparelho

apply inscrever-se

appropriate apropriado(a)

approximate aproximado(a)

April abril

architecture arquitetura

argue discutir

around ao redor; perto de; por volta de

arrive chegar

art arte

article artigo

as como

ask pedir; perguntar

aspect aspecto

at às; no, na

atmosphere atmosfera

attack atacar

attractive atraente

August agosto

aunt tia

awesome impressionante

awful horrível

B

back costas

bad mau

bandstand coreto

bank banco (instituição financeira)

barn celeiro

based on baseado(a) em; com base em

basket cesta

be ser; estar

be able to ser capaz de

be back estar de volta

beach praia

bear urso

beautiful bonito(a)

because porque

become tornar-se

bedroom quarto

before antes

beginning começo, início

behind atrás

belief crença, fé

believe acreditar

bell sino

below abaixo, seguinte

besides além disso

best melhor

bet apostar

better melhor

between entre (duas pessoas ou coisas)

big grande

bike bicicleta

bill cédula, nota

biography biografia

bird pássaro

birthday aniversário

biscuit biscoito

bite morder

blank lacuna

blind cego(a)

blue azul

board quadro

book livro

boring chato(a)

born nascer

boss chefe

both ambos(as)

box caixa

boy garoto

bracelet bracelete

branch galho

bread pão

break quebrar

breakfast café da manhã

bring trazer

brother irmão

building edifício, prédio

busy ocupado(a)

but mas

butter manteiga

buy comprar

by por; ao lado de

C

cake bolo

calculate calcular

calculator calculadora

call chamar; telefonar

camel camelo

can poder

candy doce

car carro

career carreira

carpet tapete

carrot cenoura

carry carregar, levar

cat gato

cause causar; causa

century século

ceremony cerimônia

certainly certamente

challenge desafiar; desafio

champion campeão, campeã

change mudar, trocar

charitable caridoso(a)

charming encantador(a)

chart quadro, tabela

chat bate-papo; bater papo, conversar

cheap barato(a)

check conta; assinalar; verificar

child (pl. children) criança; filho(a)

childhood infância

choice escolha

choose escolher

church igreja

circle circular

city cidade

city tour passeio pela cidade

class aula; classe

classmate colega de classe

classroom sala de aula

clean limpar

climb escalada

climbing alpinismo

clog entupir

close fechar

clothes roupas

club clube

coaching treinamento

cold frio(a)

collectively coletivamente

college faculdade

color cor

column coluna

combine combinar

come chegar; vir

Come here. Venha cá.

comfortable confortável

comic strip tirinha

comment comentário

committee comitê

common comum

community comunidade

comparative comparativo

competition competição

complete completar

completely completamente

composition produção textual; redação

computer computador

concept conceito

concerned preocupado(a)

condensed condensado(a)

condition condição

consider considerar

consist consistir

construction construção

content conteúdo

continue continuar

contracted contraído(a)

contribute contribuir

conversation conversa; conversação

cook cozinhar; cozinheiro(a)

Cool! Legal!

correct corrigir; correto(a)

cost custar

cougar puma

country país

court quadra

cousin primo(a)

cover capa

cow vaca

crazy louco(a)

credit card cartão de crédito

cross cruzar; riscar

crosswords palavras cruzadas

cry chorar; grito

cute bonitinho(a)

D

dad papai

daily diariamente

dam represa

dance dançar

dancer dançarino(a)

dangerous perigoso(a)

dark escuro(a)

dark-haired moreno(a)

date data

day dia

decide decidir

delicious delicioso(a)

describe descrever

deserve merecer

develop desenvolver

dialogue diálogo

difference diferença

difficult difícil

dig cavar

dimension dimensão

dinner jantar

direct direcionar

directions instruções, modo de preparo

disappear desaparecer

disappointment desapontamento decepção

discover descobrir

discuss discutir

diving mergulho

do fazer

docile dócil

doctor doutor(a)

dog cachorro

dollar dólar

down para baixo

downtown centro da cidade

dozen dúzia

draw desenhar

dress vestido

drink beber

drive dirigir

driver motorista

drop deixar cair, derrubar

drugstore drogaria

duck pato

during durante

E

early cedo

Earth Terra

earthquake terremoto

easy fácil

eat comer

economical econômico(a)

education educação

egg ovo

Egyptian Queen rainha do Egito

elect eleger

elementary school escola primária

emergency emergência

end fim

energetic enérgico(a); vivaz

engineer engenheiro(a)

English Inglês (disciplina escolar); inglês

enjoy gostar, apreciar

enough suficiente

enter entrar

eruption erupção

especially em especial, especialmente

establish estabelecer

even até mesmo; mesmo

evening noite

every cada; todo(a), todos(as)

everybody todo mundo, todos

exactly exatamente

example exemplo

exchange intercâmbio

exercise exercitar-se; exercício

exhibition exposição

expensive caro(a)

expert especialista

explain explicar

explanation explicação

express expressar

extra a mais

extracted from extraído(a) de

extreme sport esporte radical

eye olho

eyeglasses óculos

F

face face, rosto

fact fato, realidade

failure fracasso

fall cair

family família

famous famoso(a)

fan fã

far distante, longe

far away distante

farm fazenda

fashion moda

favorite favorito(a)

February fevereiro

feeling sentimento, sensação

few poucos(as)

fight lutar

fill preencher

find encontrar

fireworks fogos de artifício

fish pescar; peixe

flight voo

flood inundar; enchente, inundação

floor chão

flower flor

fly voar

fold dobrar

food comida

for para; por

forget esquecer

form forma; formulário

free livre

Friday sexta-feira

fridge geladeira

friend amigo(a)

friendship amizade

from de (origem)

fruit fruta

frustrated frustrado(a)

full completo(a)

full-time tempo integral

fun diversão; divertido(a)

funny engraçado(a)

future futuro

futuristic futurista

G

game jogo

garage garagem

garden jardim

gas station posto de gasolina

gate portão

Geography Geografia (disciplina escolar)

Germany Alemanha

get ficar; ganhar; obter; receber

get better melhorar

get home chegar em casa

get out sair

get up levantar-se

gift presente

girl garota

girlfriend namorada

give dar

glad alegre, contente, feliz

glass copo

glossary glossário

go ir

go out sair

goal objetivo

gold ouro; dourado(a)

good bom, boa

grade série

grammar gramática

grandfather avô

grandma vovó

grandpa vovô

grandparents avós

great ótimo(a)

group grupo

grow up crescer (tornar-se adulto)

guess adivinhar

guide guia

guitar violão

guy cara (gíria)

gym academia

H

habit hábito

hair cabelo; pelo

hamburger hambúrguer

hand mão

handsome bonito

hang-gliding asa-delta

happen acontecer

happy feliz

hard difícil, duro(a)

hate odiar

have ter

he ele

healthy saudável

hear ouvir

heat calor

help ajudar

helpful útil

her dela

here aqui

hero herói

him dele

hit bater

hold apoiar; segurar

holiday feriado; férias

home casa; lar

homework lição de casa

hope esperar, ter esperança

horror movie filme de terror

hot quente

hour hora

house casa

housewife dona de casa

how como

How long...? Por quanto tempo...?

How many...? Quantos(as)...?

How much...? Quanto custa...?

How old...? Qual a idade...?

huge enorme

hungry com fome, faminto(a)

hurt ferir, machucar

I

I eu

ice cream sorvete

idea ideia

if se

illustrate ilustrar

image imagem

imagine imaginar

important importante

impossible impossível

impressed impressionado

impressive impressionante

improve melhorar

in em, no, na

in front of em frente de

in the middle of no meio de

increase aumento, crescimento

incredible incrível

influence influenciar; influência

information informação

initiative iniciativa

inside dentro de

instructional instrucional

interest interessar; interesse

interesting interessante

interrogative interrogativa

interview entrevista

invention invenção

inventor criador(a), inventor(a)

involve envolver

involved envolvido(a)

irritate irritar

it isso; ele(a) (usado para objetos e animais)

It's amazing! É incrível!

item item

its dele(a) (usado para objetos e animais)

J

jacket jaqueta

January janeiro

Japanese japonês(esa)

jar jarra

job trabalho, emprego

join unir-se

joy alegria, contentamento

juice suco

July julho

jump pular, saltar

just somente

K

keep guardar; manter

kennel canil

key chave

kid criança

kill matar

kind tipo

kindergarten jardim de infância

kiss beijar

kitchen cozinha

know conhecer; saber

L

lab laboratório

lady senhora

lake lago

land terra

language idioma

large grande

last passado(a); último(a)

late atrasado(a); tarde

later depois, mais tarde

leader líder

leadership liderança

leading actor ator principal

leaf folha

learn aprender

leave deixar; partir

lend emprestar

less menos

let deixar, permitir

Let's go! Vamos!

Let's make a deal. Vamos fazer um acordo.

lethal letal

letter carta; letra

lettuce alface

level nível

library biblioteca

life vida

like gostar

lion leão

listen ouvir

little pequeno(a)

live morar; viver

living room sala de estar

lollipop pirulito

long longo(a), comprido(a)

look olhar; parecer

look for procurar

look like parecer

lose perder

loud em alto volume

love amar; amor

luckily felizmente

lucky sortudo(a)

lunch almoço

M

macaw arara

magazine revista

magic mágica

main principal

mainly principalmente

maintain conservar, manter

make fazer

make-up maquiagem

make sure ter certeza

male macho; masculino(a)

mall *shopping center*

man (pl. men) homem

manner maneira

many muitos(as)

map mapa

March março

market mercado

match associar; ligar, unir

Math Matemática (disciplina escolar)

May maio

may poder

maybe talvez

me me; mim

meal refeição

mean significar

meaning significado

medal medalha

media mídia

meet conhecer; encontrar

mention mencionar

message mensagem

meter metro

middle meio

military militar

milk leite

million milhão

mind mente

minute minute

miss sentir falta; perder

mission missão

mistake erro

mixture mistura

mom mãe

moment momento

Monday segunda-feira

money dinheiro

monkey macaco

month mês

more mais

morning manhã

most mais; maioria

mother mãe

mountain montanha

mouth boca

move mudar-se

movie filme

movies cinema

Mr. (Mister) sr. (senhor)

Mrs. (Miss) sra. (senhora)

much muito

museum museu

music música

must dever

my meu, minha

N

name nomear; nome

named chamado(a)

napkin guardanapo

narrative narrativo(a)

national nacional

near perto

need necessitar, precisar

negative negativo(a)

neighbor vizinho(a)

nervous nervoso(a)

never nunca

new novo(a)

news notícias; novidades

newspaper jornal

next próximo(a), seguinte

nice agradável, legal

night noite

no não

Nobel Peace Prize Prêmio Nobel da Paz

nobody ninguém

noise barulho

nominate nomear

nomination nomeação

nominee candidato(a)

northern nordeste, nortista

not não

notebook caderno

nothing nada

notice notar, perceber

novel romance

now agora

nowadays hoje em dia

number numerar; número

numerous numeroso(a)

O

o'clock em ponto

obedient obediente

object objetivo(a)

obstacle obstáculo

occupation ocupação, profissão

of de

of course lógico; claro

of the do(s), da(s)

office escritório

often frequência

oil free sem gordura

old velho(a)

on em cima de, sobre

on the left à esquerda

on the right à direita

once uma vez

only apenas

open abrir

opinion opinião

opposite oposto(a)

or ou

orange laranja

order pedir; ordenar; ordem

organization organização

organize organizar

other outro(s), outra(s)

our nosso(s), nossa(s)

over sobre

owner dono(a)

P

page página

paint pintar

painter pintor(a)

painting pintura

pan panela

paraglider parapente

paralympic paralímpico(a)

parentheses parênteses

parents pais

park parque

parking lot estacionamento

part parte

participate participar

party festa

pass passar

past passado

patient paciente

paw pata

pay pagar

peace paz

peaceful calmo(a)

pen caneta

pencil lápis

pencil case estojo

penicillin penicilina

people povo

pepper pimenta

perform atuar, desempenhar

person (pl. people) pessoa

personal pessoal

pet animal de estimação

phone telefone

physicist físico

pick up pegar

picture imagem

pie torta

pilot piloto

pink cor-de-rosa

place colocar; lugar

plan planejar; plano

plane avião

plastic plástico

plate prato

play brincar; jogar; tocar (instrumento musical); peça de teatro

player jogador(a)

playful brincalhão(ona)

playground pátio de recreio

please por favor

pleased satisfeito(a)

poetic poético(a)

police polícia

pool piscina

pop popular

pore poro

Portuguese Português (disciplina escolar); português

possible possível

post afixar, colar; publicar

postcard cartão-postal

pot pote

practice praticar, treinar

predator predador(a)

prefer preferir

prepare preparar

present apresentar; presentear

president president

prevent prevenir

private particular

prize prêmio

probably provavelmente

project projeto

promise prometer

pronoun pronome

protect proteger

protest protestar

provide fornecer

puberty puberdade

public público(a)

publication publicação

publish publicar

published publicado(a)

put colocar

Q

question pergunta, questão

quick rápido(a)

quit deixar, desistir, renunciar

R

racing corrida

rafting canoagem

rain chover

react reagir

reaction reação

read ler

reader leitor(a)

reading leitura

ready pronto(a)

realize perceber

really realmente

Really? Sério?

reappear reaparecer

reason razão

receive ganhar, receber

recipe receita

recreation recreação

red vermelho(a)

reference referência

refrigerator refrigerador, geladeira

region região

related relacionado(a)

relationship relacionamento

relatives parentes

remove remover

research pesquisar

respect respeitar; respeito

rest descansar

restaurant restaurante

review revisão

rewrite reescrever

rhino rinoceronte

rich rico(a)

ride andar a, andar de

right certo(a), direito; direita

right now agora, neste instante

risk risco

roll rolo

roller coaster montanha-russa

roof telhado

room sala

root for torcer por

rule regra

ruler régua

run correr

running corrida

S

sack saco

sad triste

safe seguro(a)

safety segurança

salad salada

sale venda

salt sal

same mesmo(a)

sandwich sanduíche

Saturday sábado

sausage salsicha

say dizer

school escola

schoolbag mochila escolar

scrub esfregar

see ver

sell vender

semester semestre

send enviar

sentence frase, sentença

several vários(as)

shake chacoalhar, sacudir

shape forma

share compartilhar

shark tubarão

she ela

shelf prateleira

shoot filmar

shopping compra(s)

short curto(a); pequeno(a)

should deveria

shoulder ombro

show exibir, mostrar; mostra

shut up calar a boca

shy tímido(a)

sick doente

side lado

sight visão

signature assinatura

silver prata

simple simples

since desde

sing cantar

singer cantor(a)

sink afundar

sister irmã

sit sentar-se

situation situação

size tamanho

skill habilidade

skin pele

skinny magro(a)

skydiving paraquedismo

sleep dormir

slow lento(a)

small pequeno(a)

snack lanche

snake cobra

so então; tão

so that para que

soccer futebol

soft drink refresco, refrigerante

some algum(ns), alguma(s); um pouco

someone alguém

something algo, alguma coisa

sometimes às vezes

song canção, música

songwriter compositor(a)

soon logo

speak falar

speech discurso

speechless pasmo(a), sem palavras

spend gastar; passar (tempo)

spoon colher

sport esporte

spread espalhar

square quadra, quarteirão

stand ficar em pé

stand up afrontar; levantar-se

standard padrão

start começar

statuette estatueta

stay ficar

step passo

still ainda

stomach estômago

stop parar

story estória; conto

street rua

student estudante

study estudar

subject matéria

substitute substituir

succeed obter sucesso

success sucesso

successful bem-sucedido(a)

suddenly de repente

sugar açúcar

suggestion sugestão

summer verão

Sunday domingo

sunscreen protetor solar

superlative superlativo

supper ceia, jantar

Sure! Com certeza!

surprised surpreso(a)

sweet doce

swim nadar

swimmer nadador(a)

swimming natação

synonym sinônimo

T

take levar; pegar; tomar

take a look dar uma olhada

talent talento

talk conversar, falar

target alvo

tea chá

teabag saquinho de chá

teach ensinar

teacher professor(a)

team time

tear lágrima

technique técnica

teen jovem

teenager adolescente

telephone telefone

tell dizer

tense tempo (verbal)

test teste, prova

text texto

than do que

that aquele(a), aquilo; que

That's scary. Que assustador.

the o(s), a(s)

the least o menos

the most o mais

theater teatro

their deles, delas

them eles, elas

then depois; então

there is / are há

these estes(as)

they eles, elas

thick grosso(a)

thin fino(a); magro(a)

thing coisa

think achar, pensar

this este(a)

those aqueles(as)

throw atirar, jogar

throw a party dar uma festa

Thursday quinta-feira

time tempo; vez

tired cansado(a)

tiring cansativo(a)

title título

today hoje

together juntos(as)

toilet paper papel higiênico

tomato tomate

tomorrow amanhã

tonight hoje à noite

too também

touch tocar

toward em direção a

tower torre

town cidade

toy brinquedo

traditional tradicional

traffic trânsito

train treinar; trem

trash lixo

travel viajar

treatment tratamento

tree árvore

trip viagem

trouble dificuldade

true verdadeiro(a)

truth verdade

try tentar

Tuesday terça-feira

turn on ligar

TV televisão

twice duas vezes

U

ugly feio(a)

unbelievable inacreditável

uncle tio

under embaixo de, sob

undergo submeter-se

underline sublinhar

understand entender

unhappy infeliz

uniform uniforme

unique único(a)

unit unidade

university universidade

unscramble desembaralhar

until até

up to por até

upset chateado(a)

urban urbano

urban designer urbanista

us nós

use usar

used usado(a)

usually geralmente

V

vacation férias

vaccine vacina

vanilla baunilha

vegetable vegetal

verb verbo

very muito

vision visão

visit visitar

vocabulary vocabulário

volcano vulcão

volleyball voleibol

W

wait esperar

wake up acordar

walk andar, caminhar; passear

wall parede

want querer

wash lavar

washing machine máquina de lavar

watch assistir

water molhar, regar; água

way caminho

we nós

weak fraco(a)

wear usar, vestir

weather clima

wedding ceremony cerimônia de casamento

Wednesday quarta-feira

week semana

weekday dia da semana

weekend fim de semana

welcome bem-vindo(a)

well bem

what o que, que, qual

What about…? Que tal…?

What time…? Que horas…?

when quando

where onde

while enquanto; embora

who quem

whole inteiro(a); todo(a)

why por que, por quê

win ganhar, vencer

wind vento

winner vencedor(a)

wish desejar

with com

without sem

woman (pl. women) mulher

wood madeira

word palavra

wordsearch caça-palavras

work trabalhar; trabalho

workbook caderno de exercícios

world mundo; mundial

worse pior

write escrever

writer escritor(a)

wrong errado(a)

Y

yard quintal

Yeah! Sim!

year ano

year old ano de idade

yes sim

yesterday ontem

you você(s)

young jovem

your seu(s), sua(s)

yourself si mesmo(a)

Z

zoo zoológico

Irregular Verbs

Infinitive	Simple Past	Past Participle	Translation
be	was / were	been	ser; estar
be able to	was able to	been able to	ser capaz de
become	became	become	tornar-se
bet	bet	bet	apostar
bite	bit	bitten	morder
break	broke	broken	quebrar
bring	brought	brought	trazer
buy	bought	bought	comprar
choose	chose	chosen	escolher
come	came	come	chegar; vir
cost	cost	cost	custar
dig	dug	dug	cavar
do	did	done	fazer
draw	drew	drawn	desenhar
drink	drank	drunk	beber
drive	drove	driven	dirigir
eat	ate	eaten	comer
fall	fell	fallen	cair
feel	felt	felt	sentir(-se)
fight	fought	fought	lutar, brigar
find	found	found	encontrar
fly	flew	flown	voar
forget	forgot	forgot / forgotten	esquecer
get	got	got / gotten	ficar; ganhar; obter; receber
give	gave	given	dar
go	went	gone	ir
have	had	had	ter
hold	held	held	apoiar; segurar
hurt	hurt	hurt	ferir, machucar
keep	kept	kept	manter; ficar
know	knew	known	conhecer; saber
leave	left	left	deixar; partir
lend	lent	lent	emprestar
let	let	let	deixar, permitir

Infinitive	Simple Past	Past Participle	Translation
lose	lost	lost	perder
make	made	made	fazer
mean	meant	meant	significar
meet	met	met	conhecer; encontrar(-se)
pay	paid	paid	pagar
put	put	put	pôr, colocar
read	read	read	ler
ride	rode	ridden	andar a, andar de
run	ran	run	correr
say	said	said	dizer, falar
see	saw	seen	ver
seek	sought	sought	procurar
sell	sold	sold	vender
send	sent	sent	enviar
shoot	shot	shot	filmar
show	showed	shown	exibir, mostrar; demonstrar
sing	sang	sung	cantar
sit	sat	sat	sentar(-se)
sleep	slept	slept	dormir
speak	spoke	spoken	falar
spend	spent	spent	gastar dinheiro; passar o tempo
spread	spread	spread	espalhar
swim	swam	swum	nadar
take	took	taken	levar; pegar; tomar
teach	taught	taught	ensinar
tell	told	told	dizer, contar
think	thought	thought	achar, pensar
throw	threw	thrown	atirar
undergo	underwent	undergone	submeter-se
understand	understood	understood	entender
wake up	woke up	woken up	acordar
wear	wore	worn	usar, vestir
win	won	won	ganhar, vencer
write	wrote	written	escrever

Track List

Track	Page	Unit	Exercise
1	Introduction		
2	7	Welcome Unit	5
3	8	1	2
4	13	1	13
5	13	1	14
6	15	1	Key Language
7	18	2	2
8	23	2	9
9	25	2	Key Language
10	27	2	4
11	28	3	2
12	31	3	10
13	31	3	11
14	35	3	Key Language
15	38	4	2
16	43	4	11
17	45	4	Key Language
18	48	5	2
19	52	5	9
20	55	5	Key Language
21	58	6	2
22	63	6	14
23	65	6	Key Language
24	67	6	3
25	68	7	2
26	72	7	8
27	75	7	Key Language
28	78	8	2
29	80	8	7
30	85	8	Key Language